The Grand Ca[nal]

This is one of the most famous and popular sights in the world. The Grand Canal is easily recognisable, but here there is a slight twist: painting it by night allows you to create exciting colour markings and dazzling contrasts.

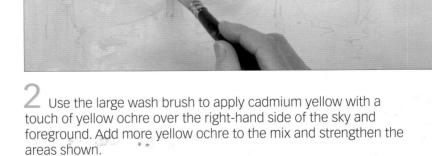

1 Transfer the image on to watercolour paper as shown opposite, and secure it to the board with masking tape.

2 Use the large wash brush to apply cadmium yellow with a touch of yellow ochre over the right-hand side of the sky and foreground. Add more yellow ochre to the mix and strengthen the areas shown.

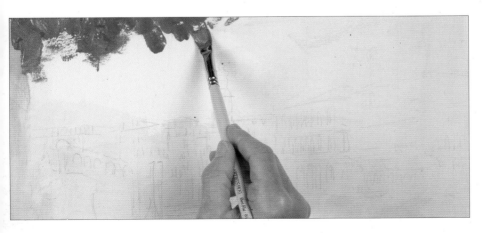

3 Make a mix of titanium white, dioxazine violet and French ultramarine. Use the hog hair size 6 short flat brush to block in the sky roughly, starting from the top left. As you work to the right, vary the quantities slightly, adding more titanium white and dioxazine violet to the mix.

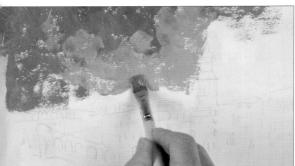

4 Add more white as you work down towards the horizon.

5 Continue painting the sky using the same mixes, working all the way over to the right.

6 Use short horizontal strokes of the same colours to begin the water, leaving yellow showing through in areas to represent the reflections and highlights on the water.

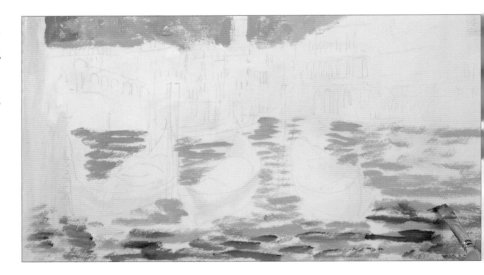

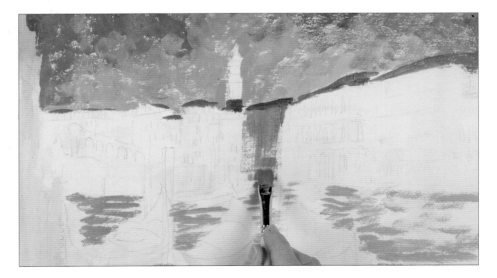

7 Make a thick mix of yellow ochre and burnt sienna with a touch of dioxazine violet, and paint in the skyline with the edge of the brush.

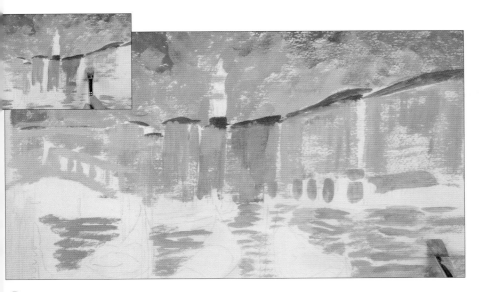

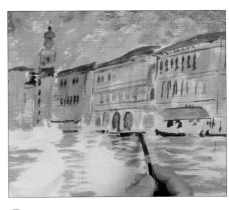

9 Add some darks with a mix of dioxazine violet and burnt sienna and the tip of the sword-liner. Use the same mix of paints to start hinting at structure in the buildings.

8 Add titanium white to the mix and draw the paint down the fronts of the buildings (see inset), then add touches of French ultramarine and dioxazine violet and block in the reflections of the buildings.

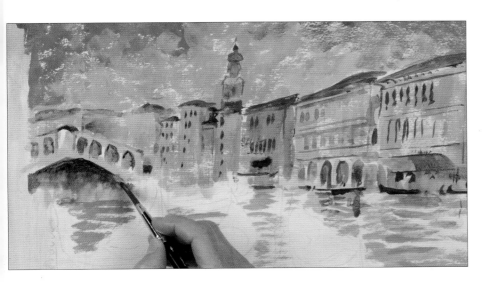

10 Continue blocking in details with the same colour mix, paying particular attention to the Rialto Bridge.

11 Switch to the hog hair size 2 short flat brush and use a mixture of burnt umber and dioxazine violet to block in the right-most boat. Add French ultramarine and titanium white to the mix to paint the tarpaulin.

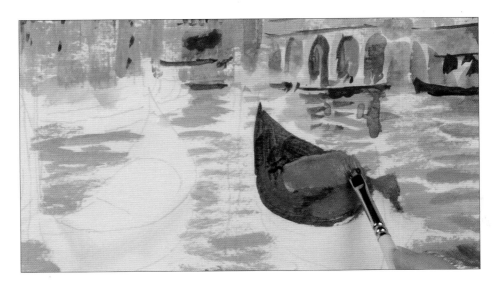

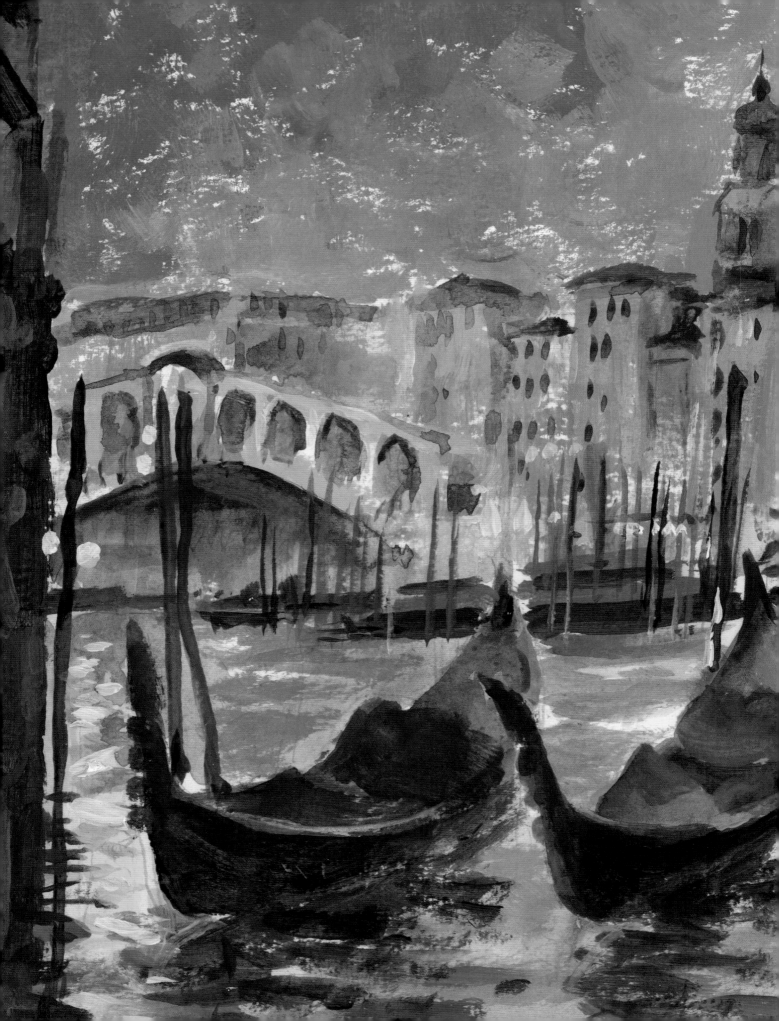

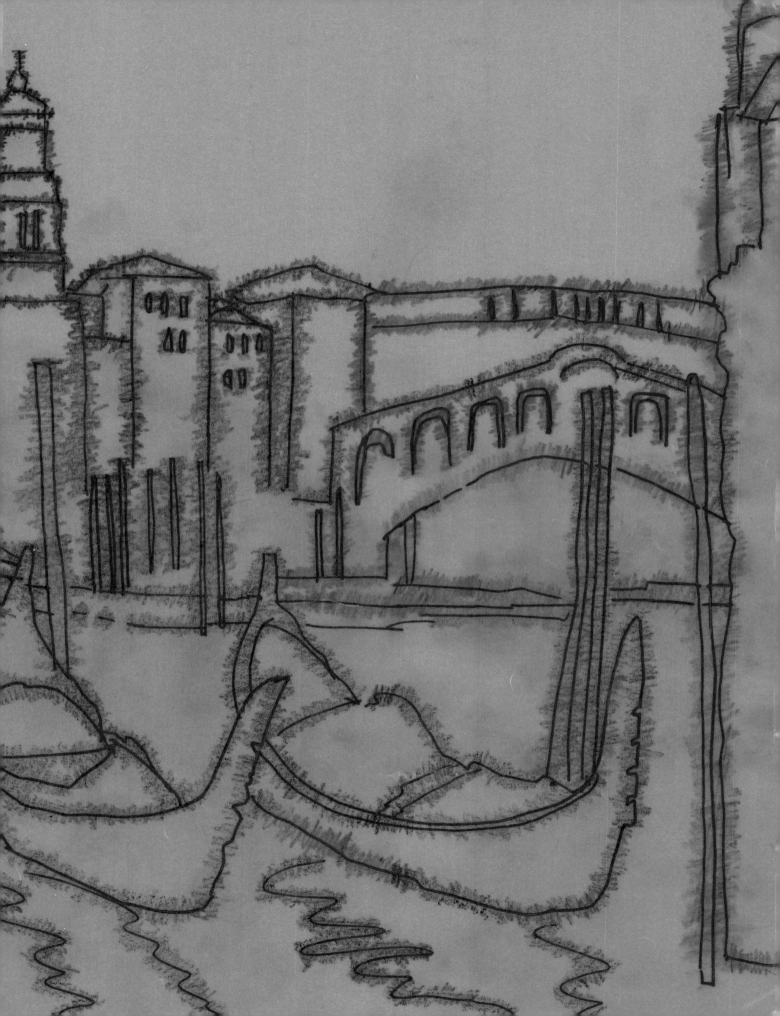

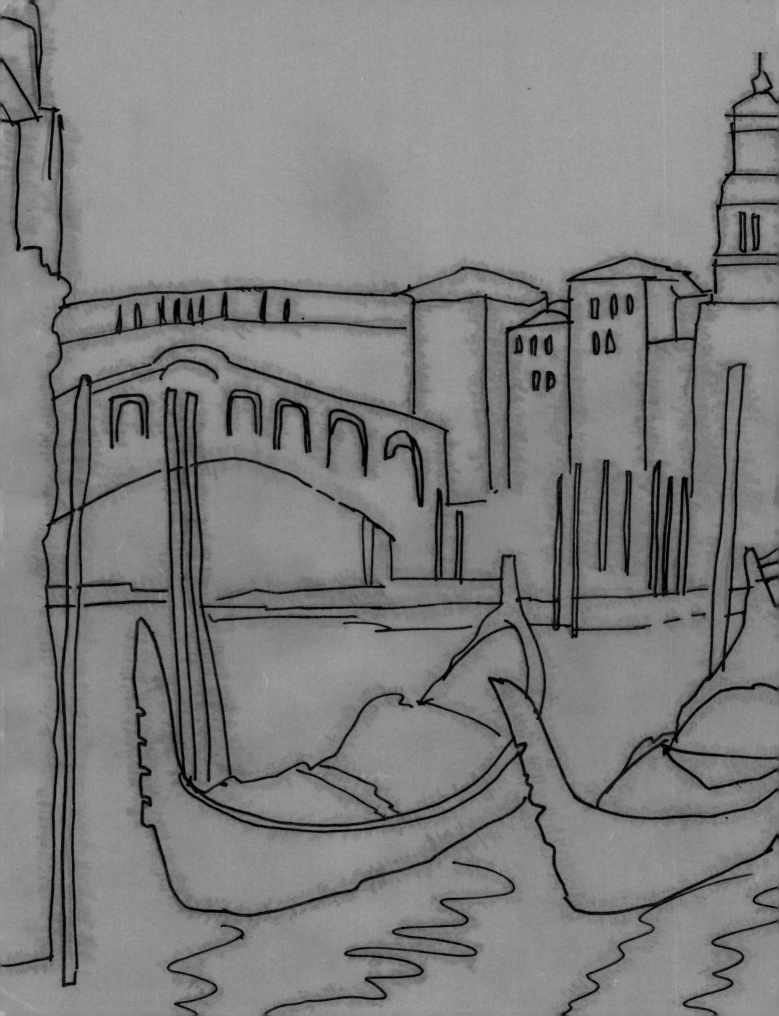

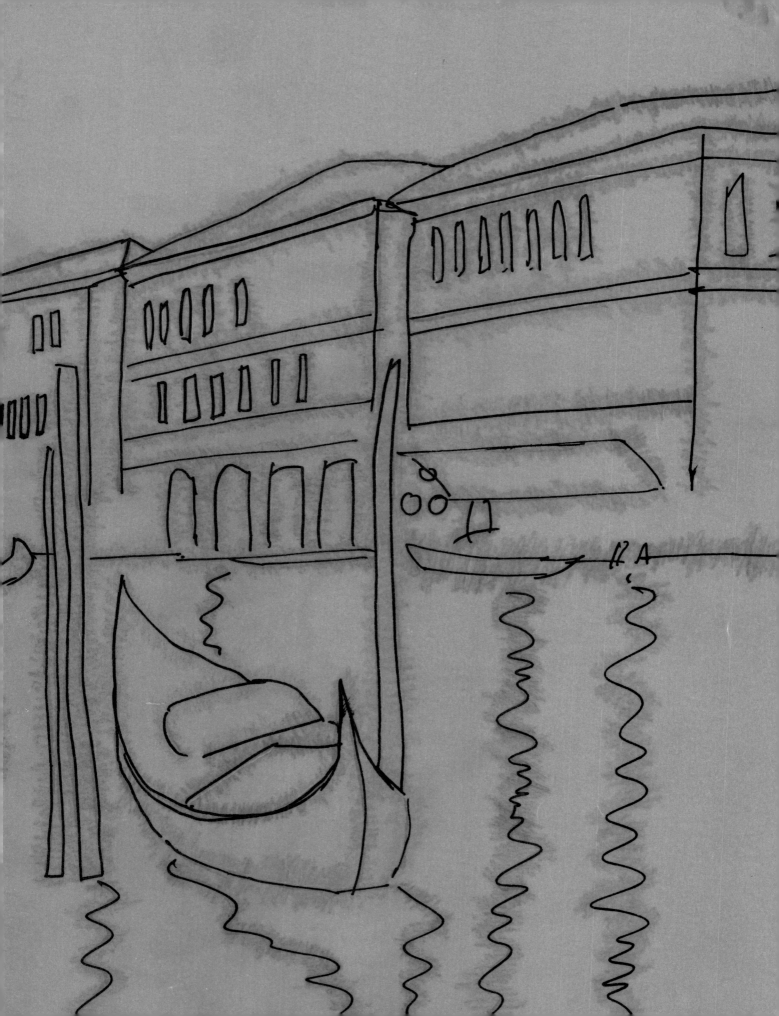

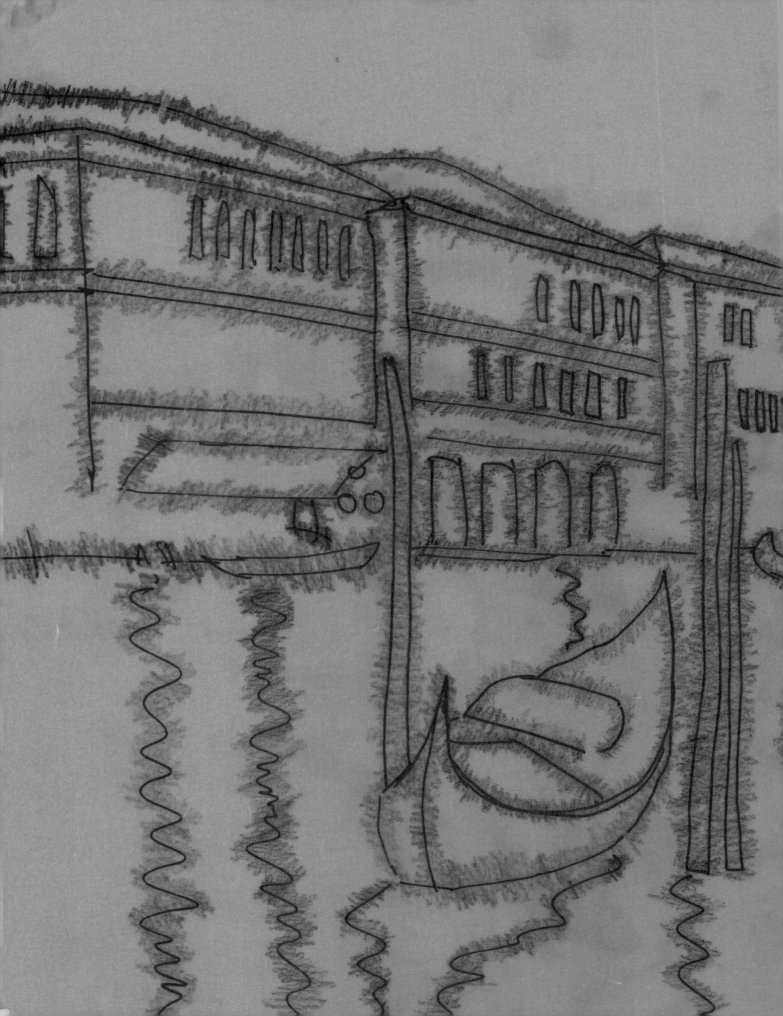

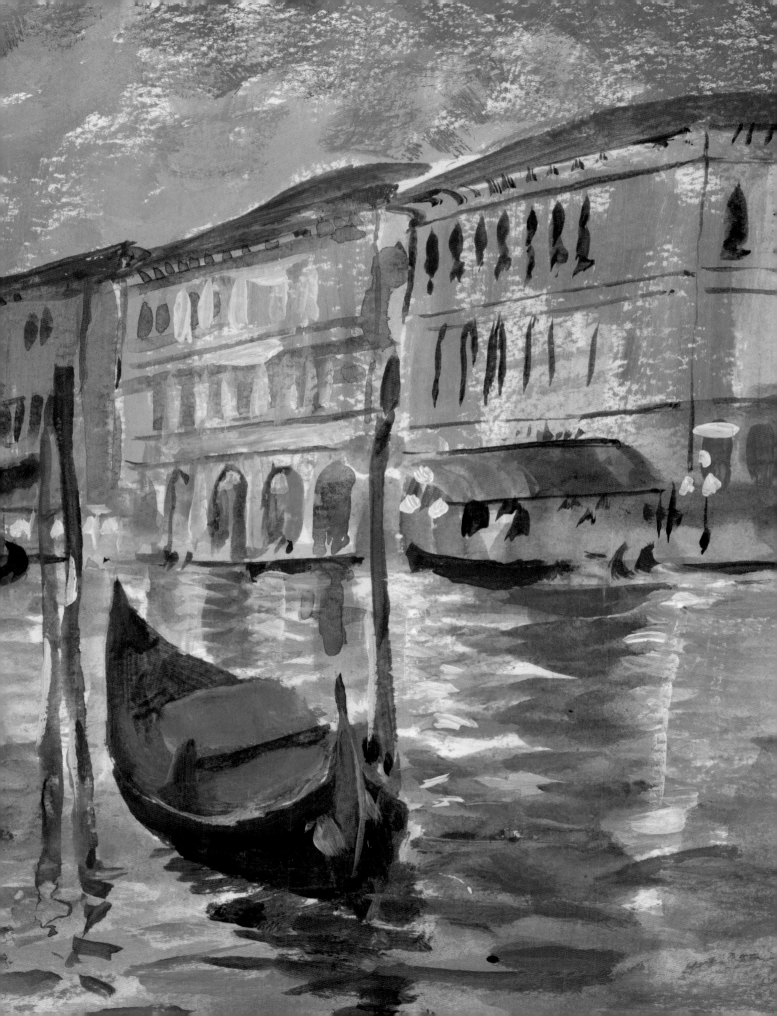

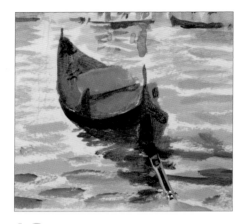

12 Return to the original mix of burnt umber and dioxazine violet to paint the outside of the boat and reflections.

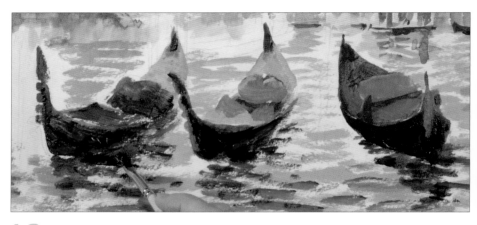

13 Paint the other boats with similar colour mixes, varying the amount of the different paints in the mix to make some natural-looking variations.

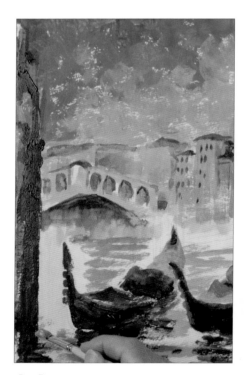

14 Glaze dilute burnt sienna over the left-hand side, then add French ultramarine and burnt sienna over the top.

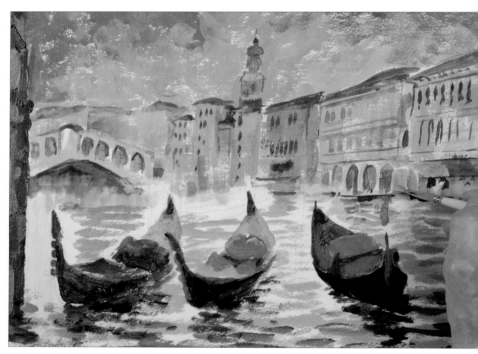

15 Add patches of yellow ochre in the same area, and then add yellow ochre highlights here and there on the buildings.

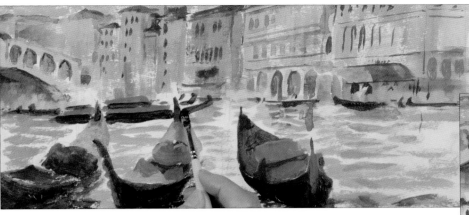

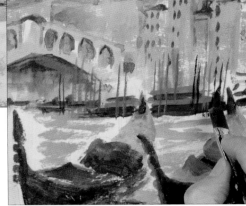

16 Paint the boats in the distance with a mix of dioxazine violet, titanium white and French ultramarine. Add more dioxazine violet and burnt sienna to the mix for shading.

17 Switch to the sword-liner and use the tip to add the poles with a mix of dioxazine violet, titanium white and a touch of burnt sienna; then shade them with a mix of burnt sienna and French ultramarine.

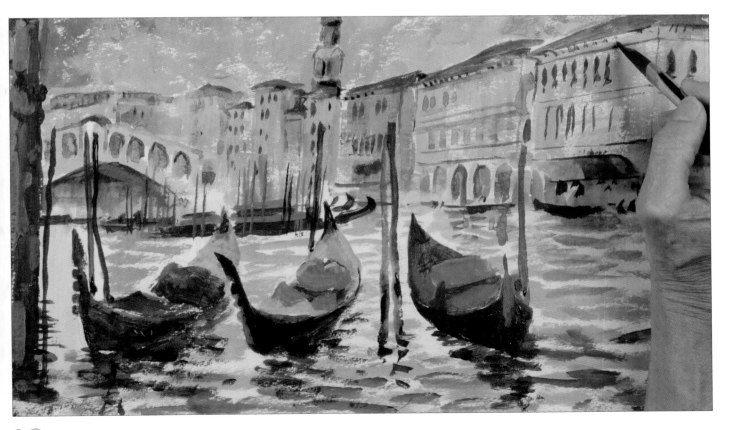

18 Add the poles in the foreground with a darker shade of the same mixes, then use the same colour to add details to the buildings in the background.

19 Use a mix of cadmium orange and cadmium yellow to add street lighting and the reflections. Add the same highlights to the boats where the light catches them. You can use phthalo blue (green shade) to knock back any yellow in the water that is too strong.

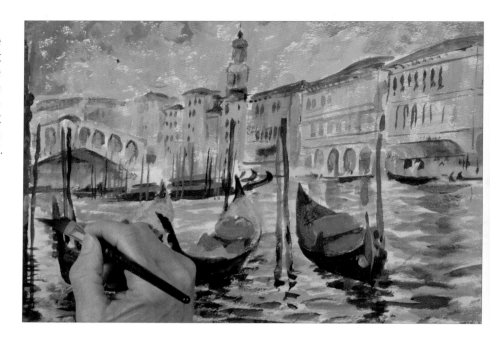

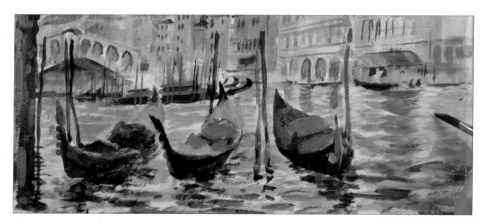

20 Add pure cadmium yellow on the water where shafts of light hit it.

21 Glaze the bottom edge of the paper with dilute French ultramarine, then add pure titanium white lights as shown.

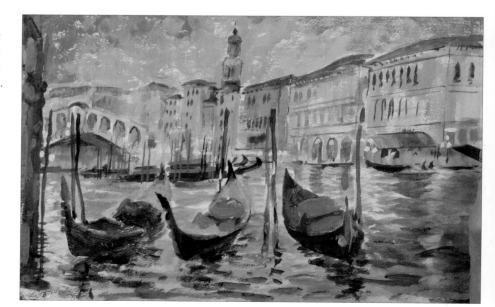

ISLE OF WIGHT

Halswood

ADDRESS BOOK

Published by Halswood Stationers

British Library Cataloguing-in-Publication Data
A CIP record for this title is available
from the British Library

ISBN 978 0 85717 014 9

HALSWOOD STATIONERS
Halsgrove House,
Ryelands Industrial Estate,
Bagley Road, Wellington, Somerset TA21 9PZ
Tel: 01823 653777   Fax: 01823 216796
email: sales@halsgrove.com

Part of the Halsgrove group of companies
Information on all Halsgrove titles is available at:
www.halsgrove.com

Printed and bound in China by
Toppan Leefung Printing Ltd (0)

Front cover: The last light of the day on the cliffs of
Freshwater Bay with pink hues on the clouds in the sky.

Back cover: A moored sailing yacht in Newtown Creek
before dawn with mist rising.

Title page: A colourful sky at dusk reflected in the wet sand
on the beach at Hanover Point, on the west of the island.

Right: Pennant flags on the stays of a classic yacht moored in
Yarmouth harbour for the Old Gaffers yacht regatta.

Overleaf: Looking out towards Niton Down over hay bales
lit by early morning light and mist covering the valley floor.

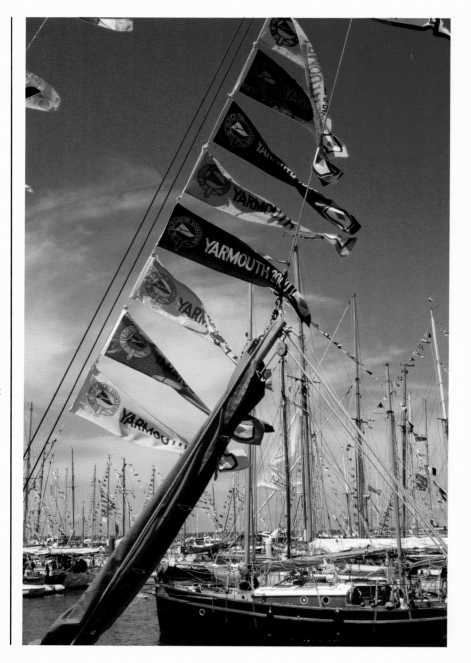

YOUR ADDRESS BOOK

The Isle of Wight has one of the most attractive and diverse landscapes in the country, in barely 380 sq km: not for nothing is it known as England in miniature.

The varied coastline ranges from rocky outcrops and high cliffs in the west to the vast sandy beaches in the east which are favoured by families with their buckets and spades. Its sheltered harbours have made it a Mecca for yachting, an intrinsic part of island life that attracts many hundreds of thousands of visitors a year, with Cowes Week being an event of international importance. Although the island's biggest industry is tourism, it is still significantly agricultural, with its inland downs sustaining sheep and dairy farming and the growing of arable crops, as well as offering stunning views. With its many historical sites, together with the strategic and interesting towns of Ryde, Sandown, Ventnor, Newport and Cowes, this means that the island in all its aspects remains a visual feast.

Master-photographer Ian Badley grew up overlooking the Needles and from his earliest years was fascinated by the Isle of Wight, intrigued by the ethereal mists that appeared to hang over the island, providing an additional dimension to its bright chalk cliffs. His sense of place and of the enchantment and beauty of each scene is evident again and again in the superb images reproduced here.

Address books tend to be well used and have a long life. Along with important contact details, they keep track of the user's friends and acquaintances, tracing their lives over time and from place to place. And, if properly attended to, an address book eventually becomes a journal in itself, and an attractive and permanent keepsake. Whether bought as a gift or for personal use, this Isle of Wight Address Book, with its superb pictorial reminders of the island, will provide years of pleasure.

USEFUL ADDRESSES AND TELEPHONE NUMBERS

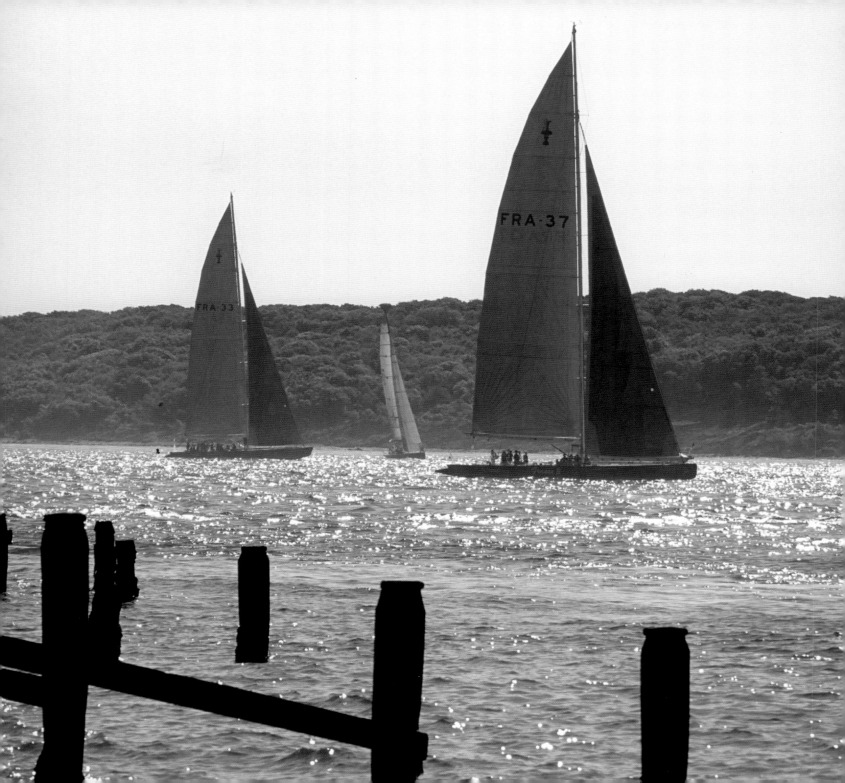

A

Tall sailing yachts making way through the western approaches of the Solent during the annual Round the Island yacht race.

A

Sandown Bay across the mist covered River Yar valley streaked by early
morning sunlight. In the distance you can see a large ship anchored.

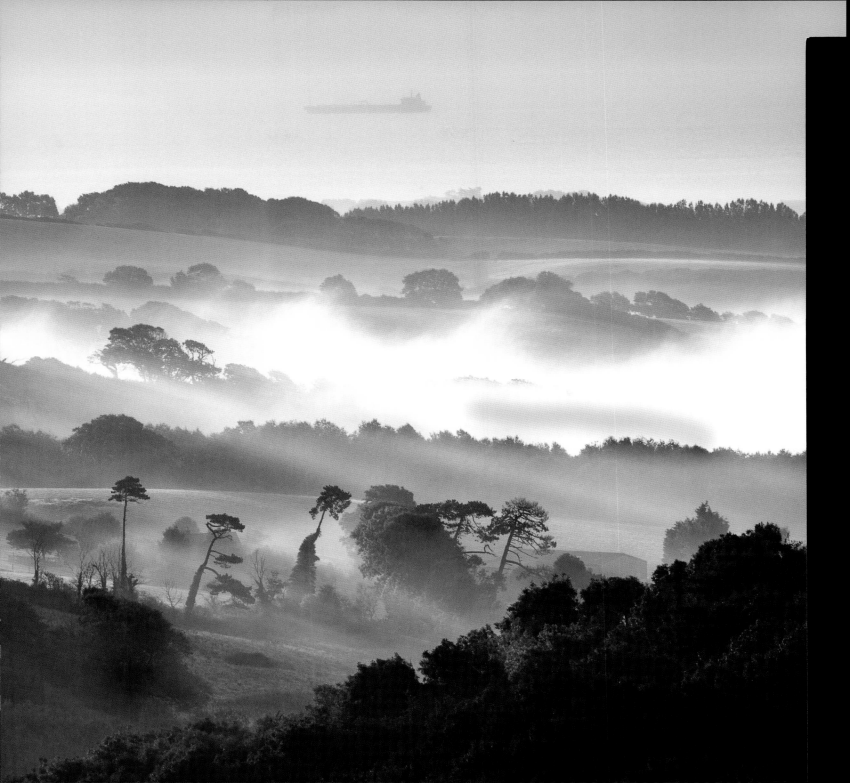

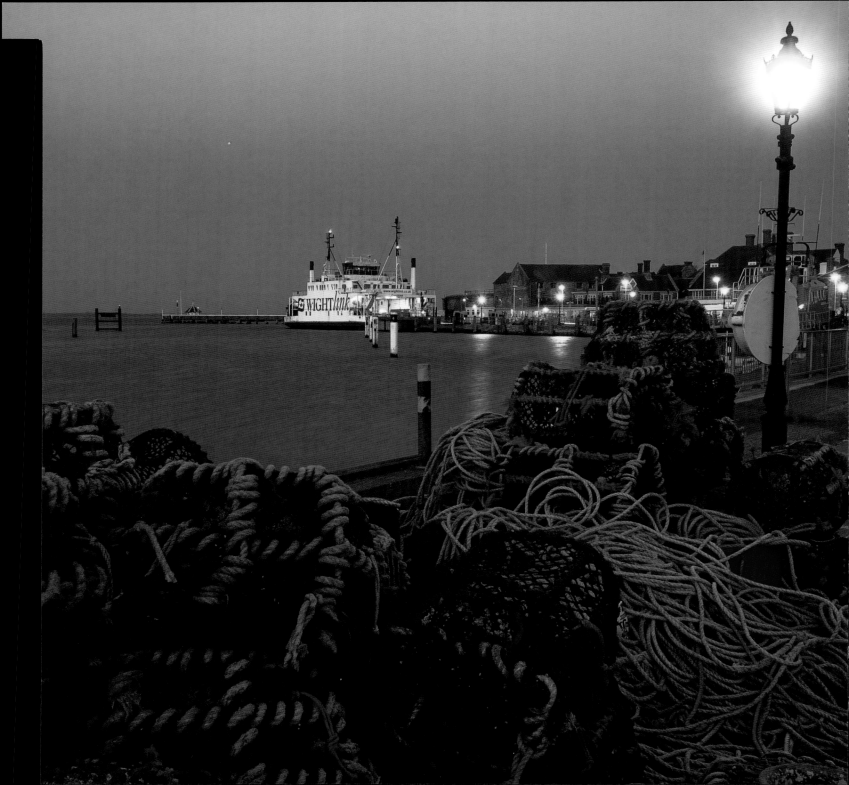

B

Lobster pots on the quay at Yarmouth with the ferry berth at dusk.
Yarmouth is a busy local port for fishermen, visiting yachtsman and the
thousands of visitors using the Lymington to Yarmouth ferry.

B

B

B

Striped deck chairs on the beach at Shanklin,
with people swimming in the sea.

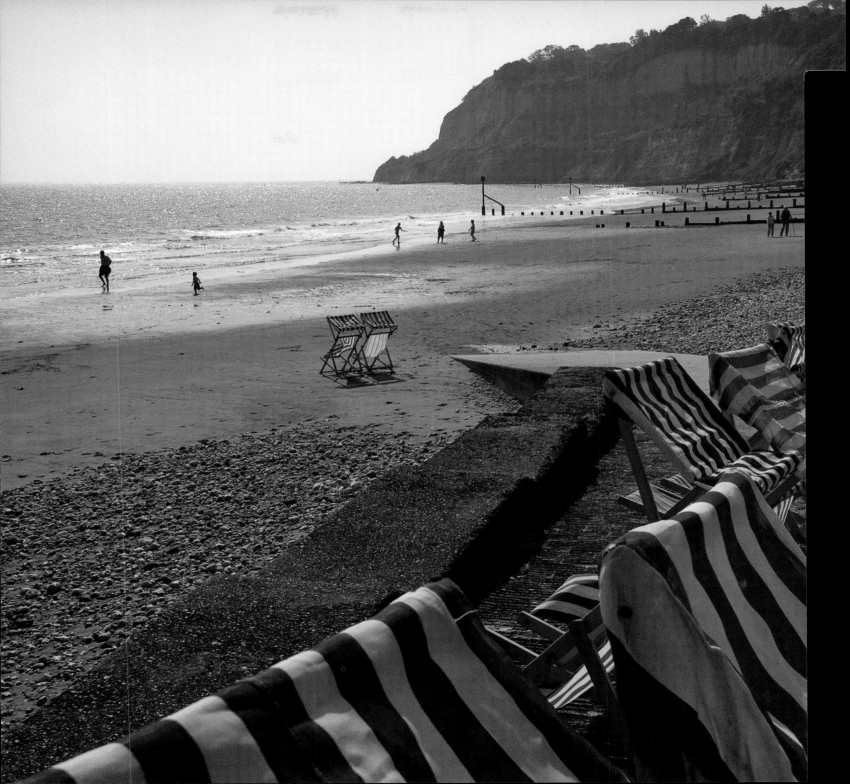

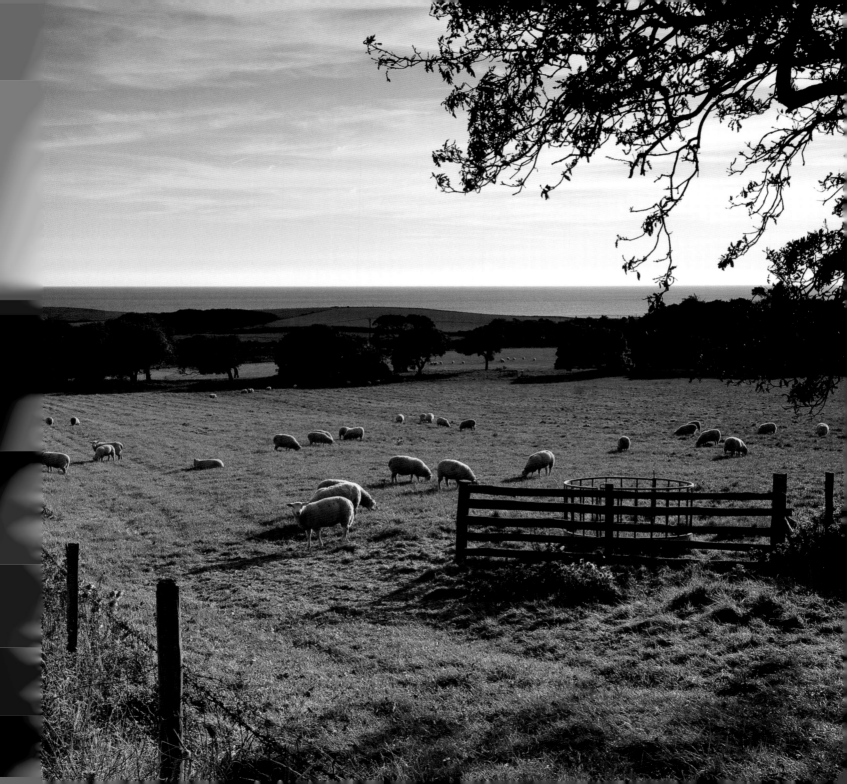

C

Sheep fields near Roughland Cliff.

C

C

C

Weed-covered rocks at low tide on
Brook Bay as the sun sets.

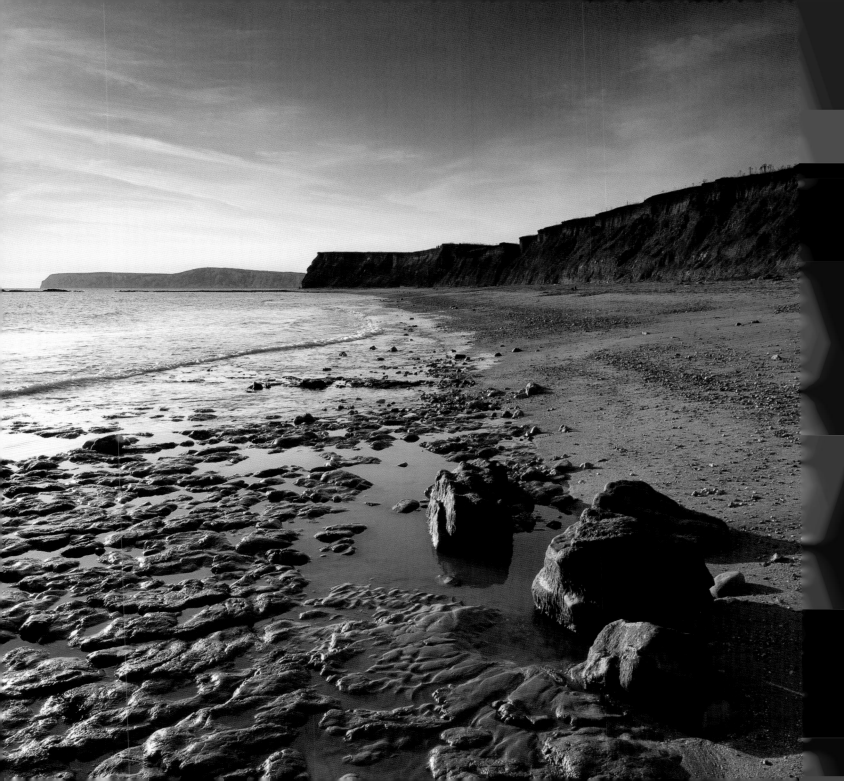

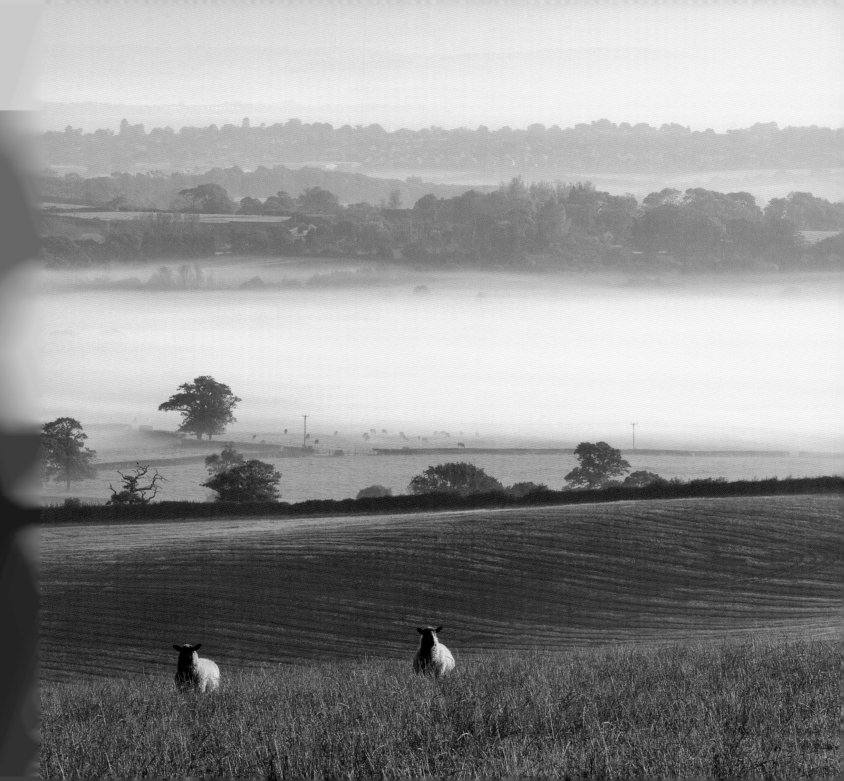

D

Two sheep grazing on Mersley Down with
low lying mist in the valley beyond.

D

D

D

A warm setting sun lights the yellow cliffs which are reflected in the rock pools at low tide. Here you can see the strata in the cliffs and many people look around the beach here for fossils.

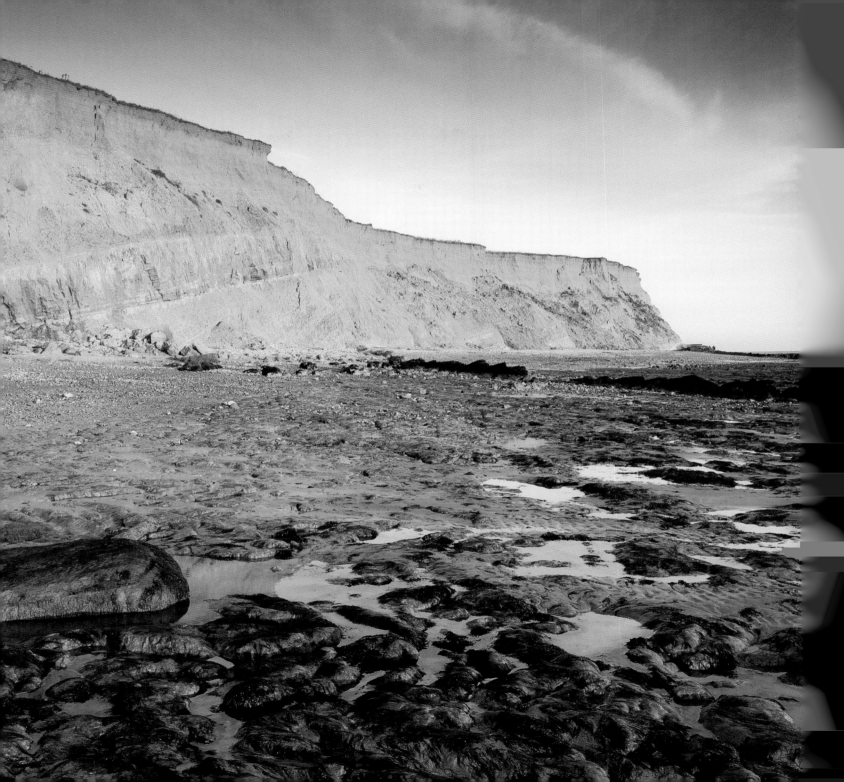

E

A colourful sky at dusk reflected in the wet sand and rock pools
on the beach at Hanover Point, on the west coast of the island.

E

E

E

Looking out towards Sandown Bay with wild flowers
in the foreground and mist streaked with sunlight in
the valley of the Yar River Trail near Newchurch.

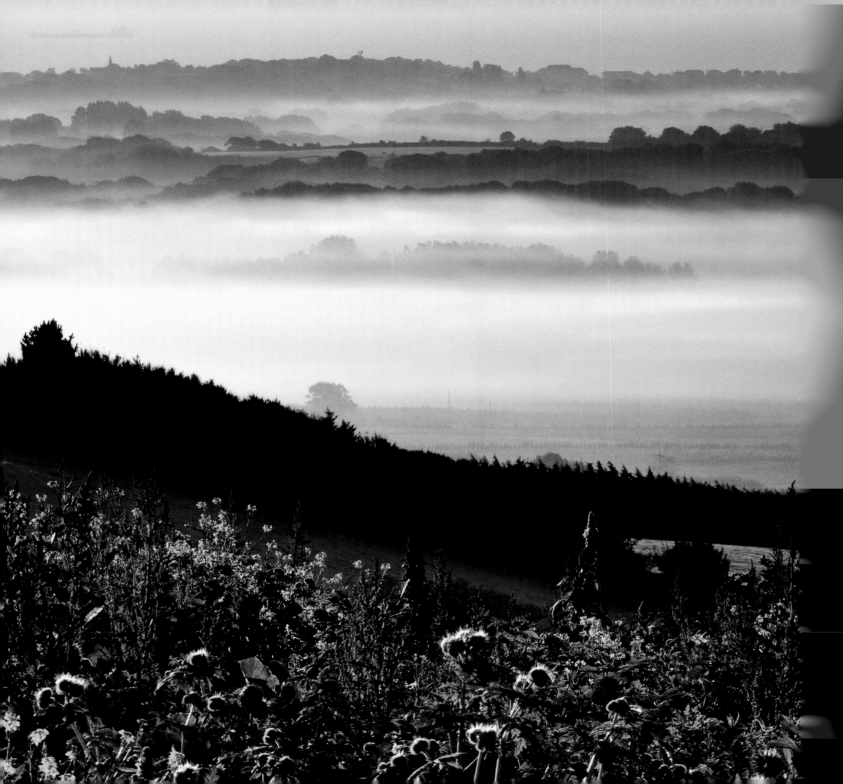

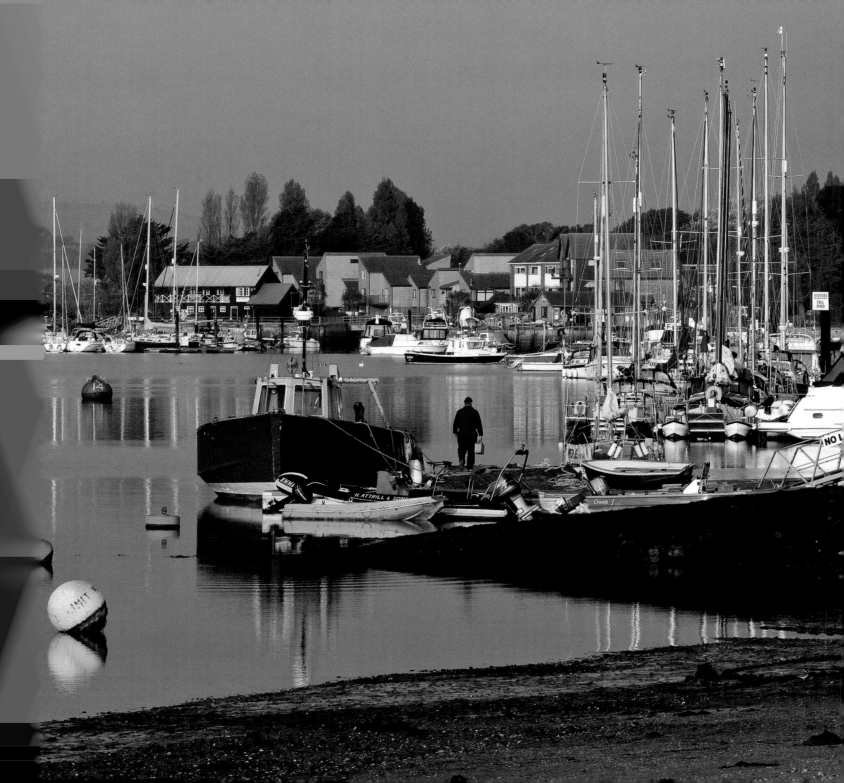

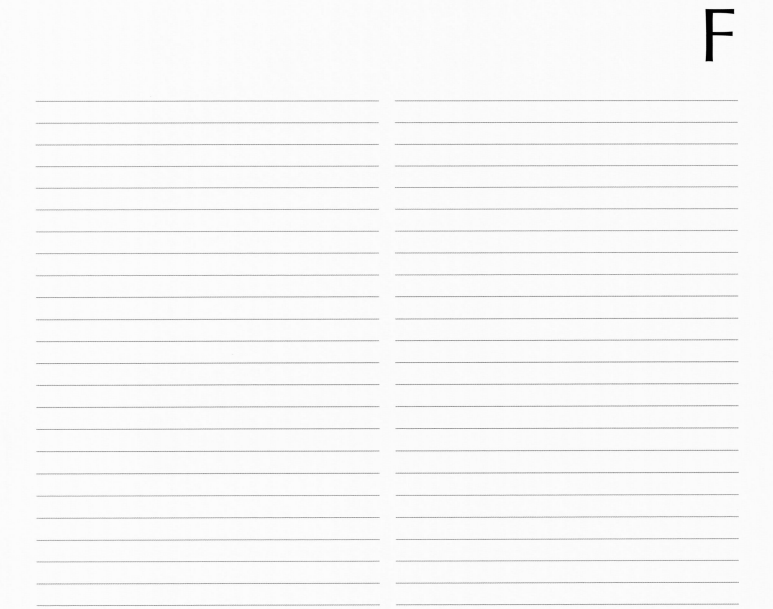

F

A fisherman walking towards his fishing
boat moored at Bembridge harbour.

F

F

F

Low tide at sunset with a view towards the
coastguard cottages at Brook Green.

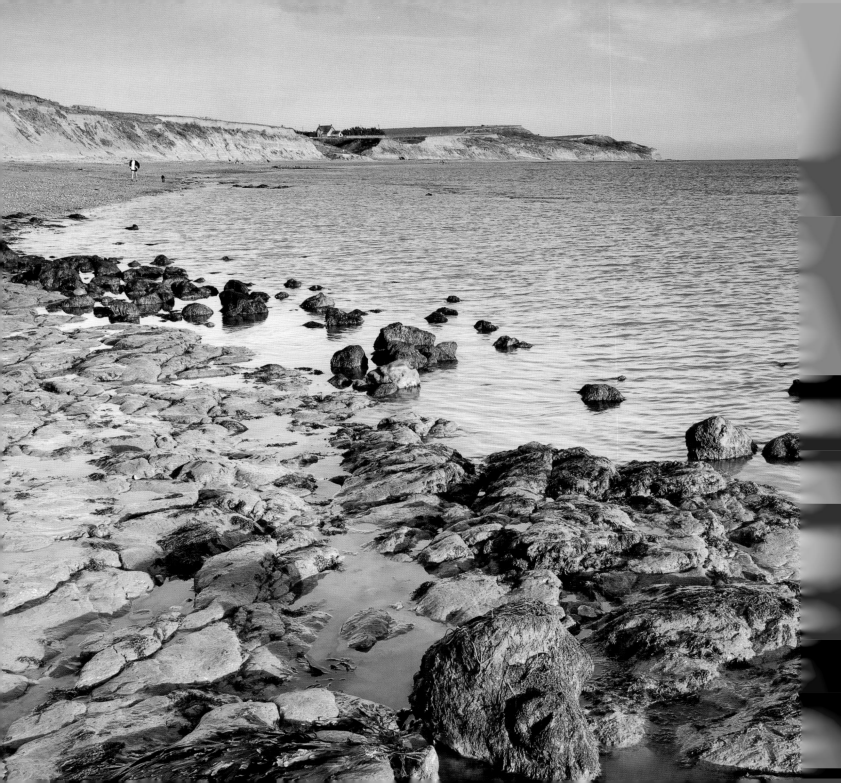

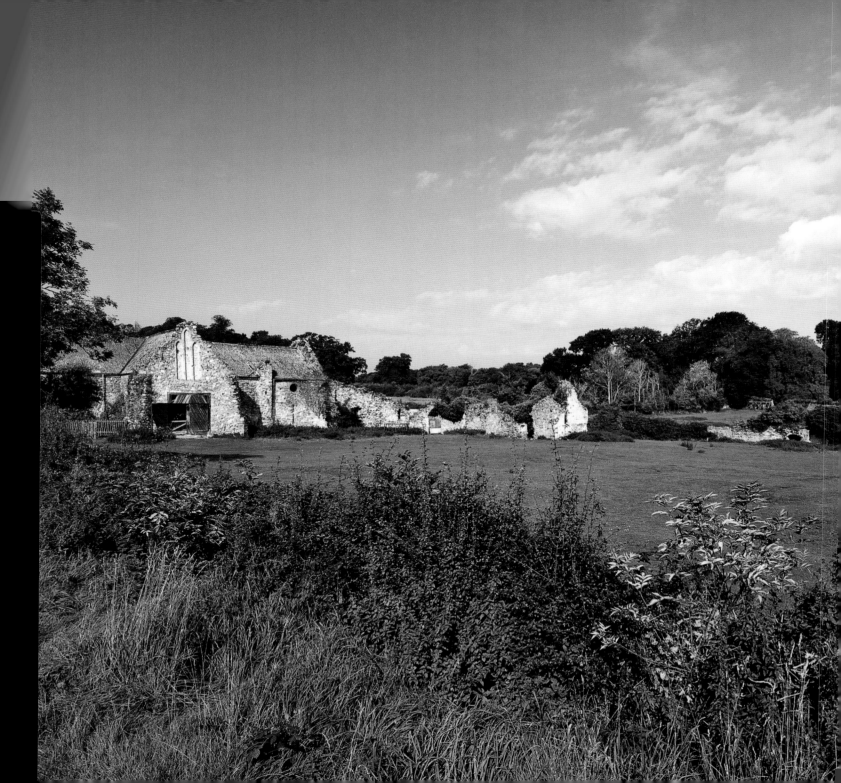

The ruins of the Cistercian abbey near Quarr Abbey, Ryde.

G

G

G

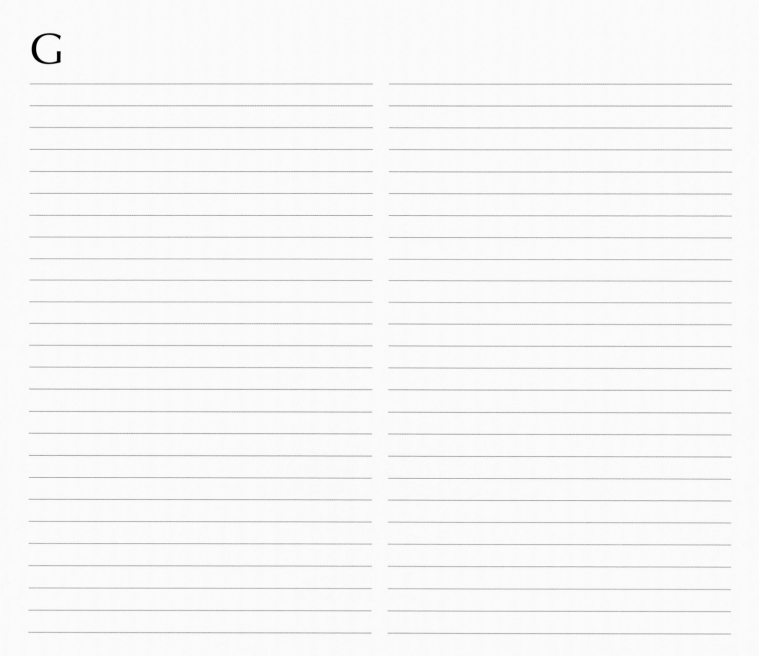

Looking towards the white cliffs of Tennyson Down from Stenbury Down.

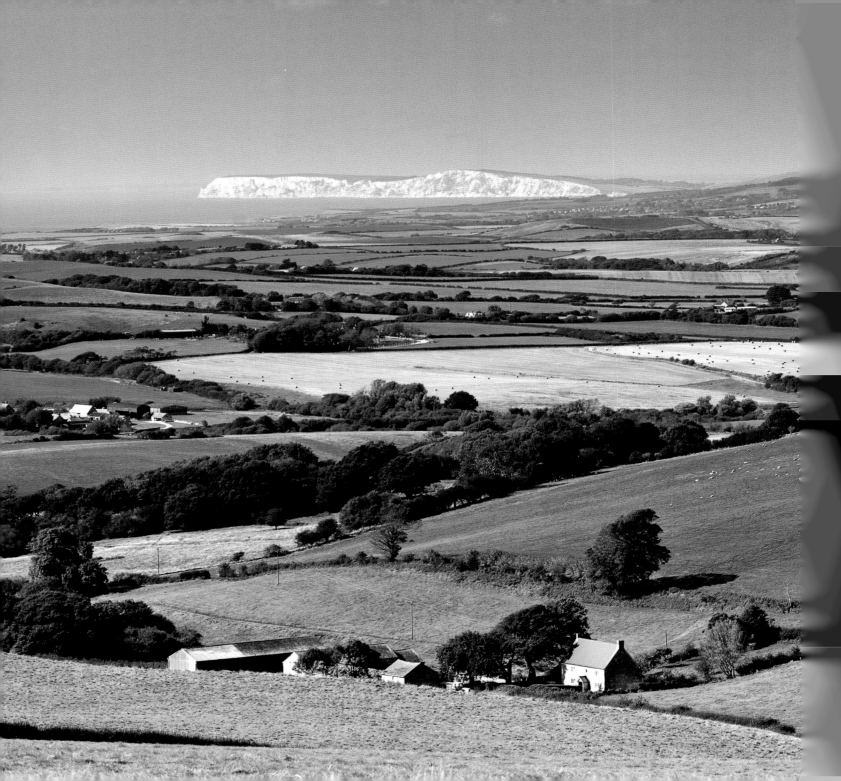

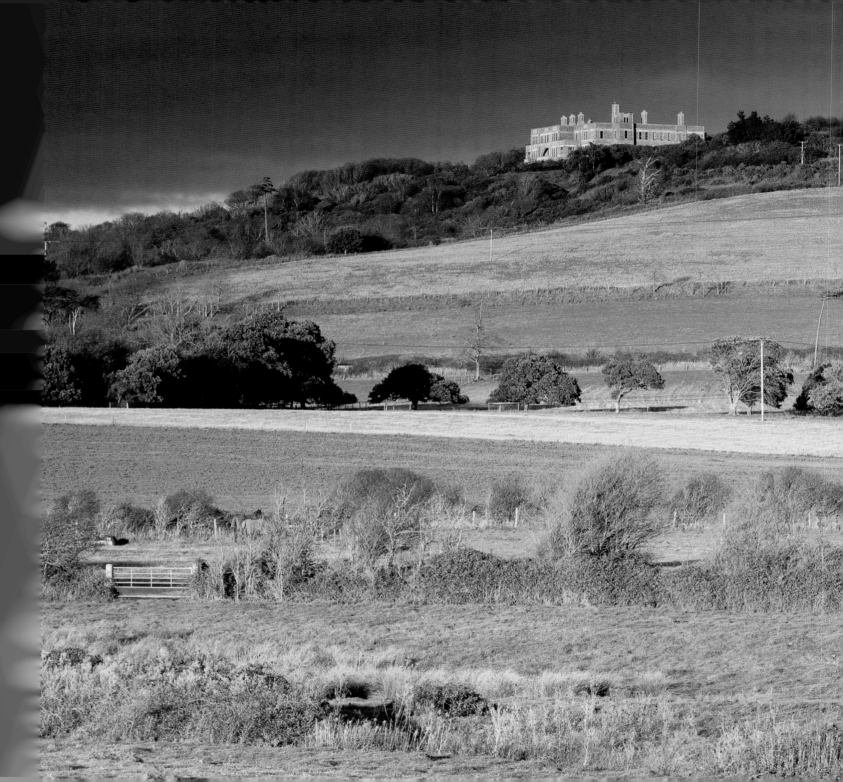

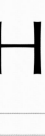

H

Late afternoon sun lights Brook Hill House, with dark storm clouds beyond. JB Priestley lived at Brook Hill House in the late 1940s having moved there from nearby Chale Green.

H

H

H

The view to All Saints' Church at Godshill with the famous
thatched cottages surrounding the green in the foreground.

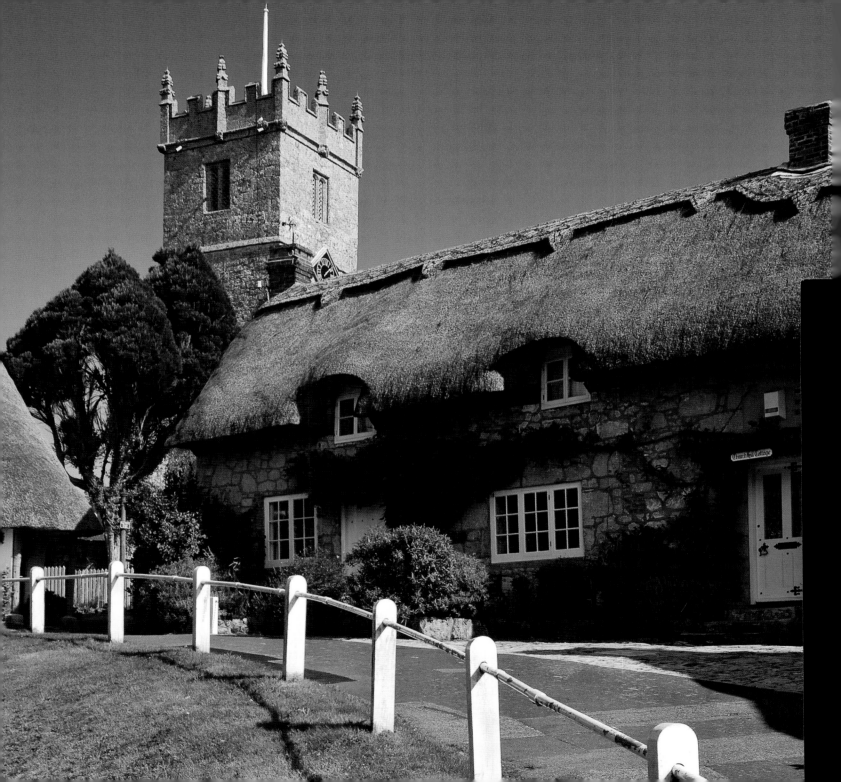

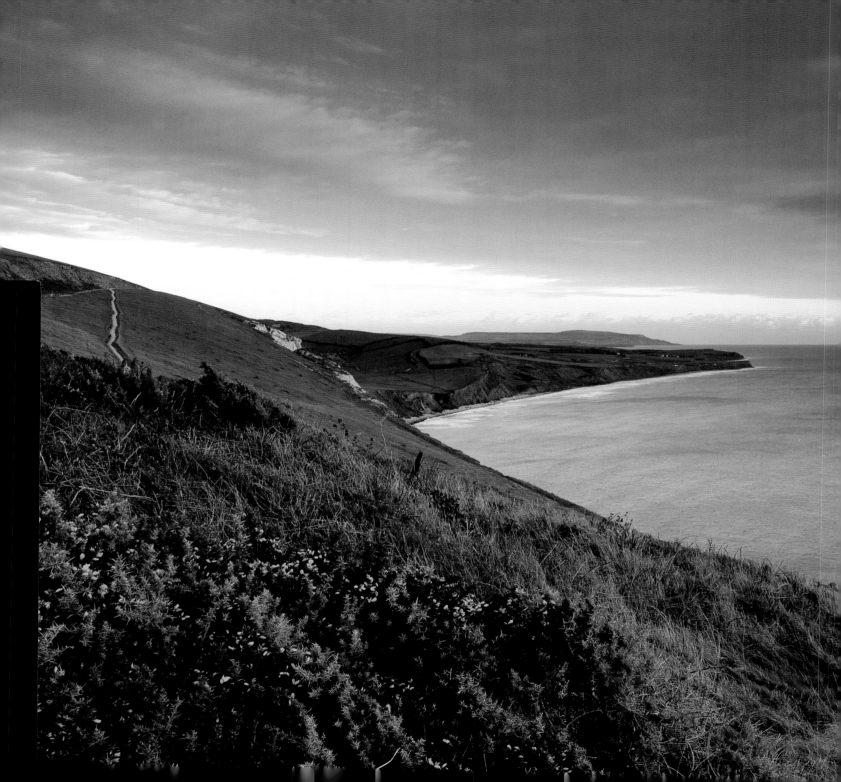

The view south from Compton Down along the
coastal footpath towards St Catherine's Hill.

|

The last light of the day on the cliffs of Freshwater
Bay with pink hues on the clouds in the sky.

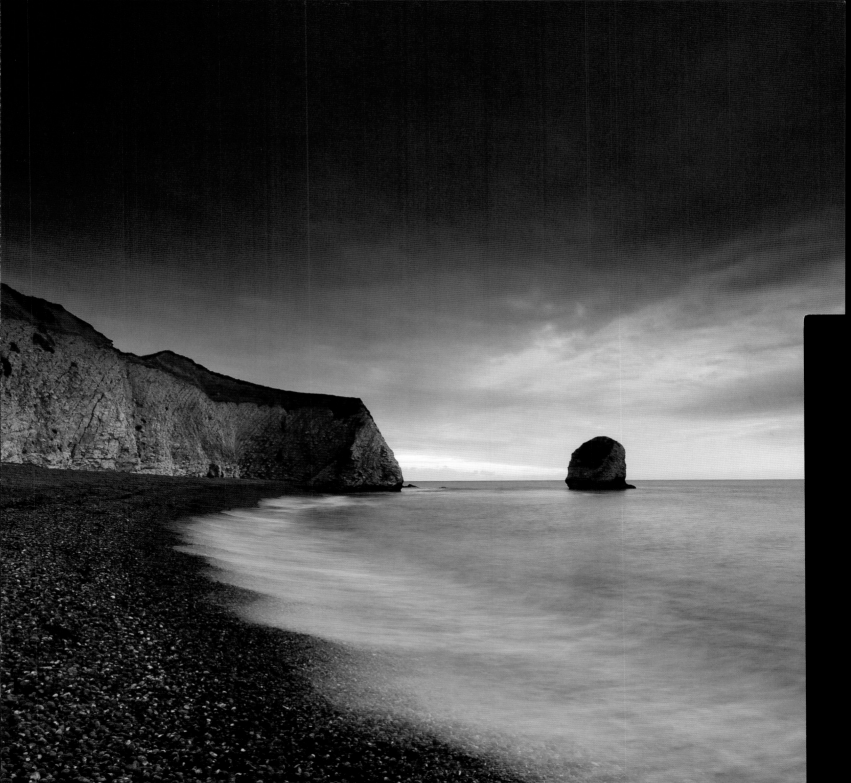

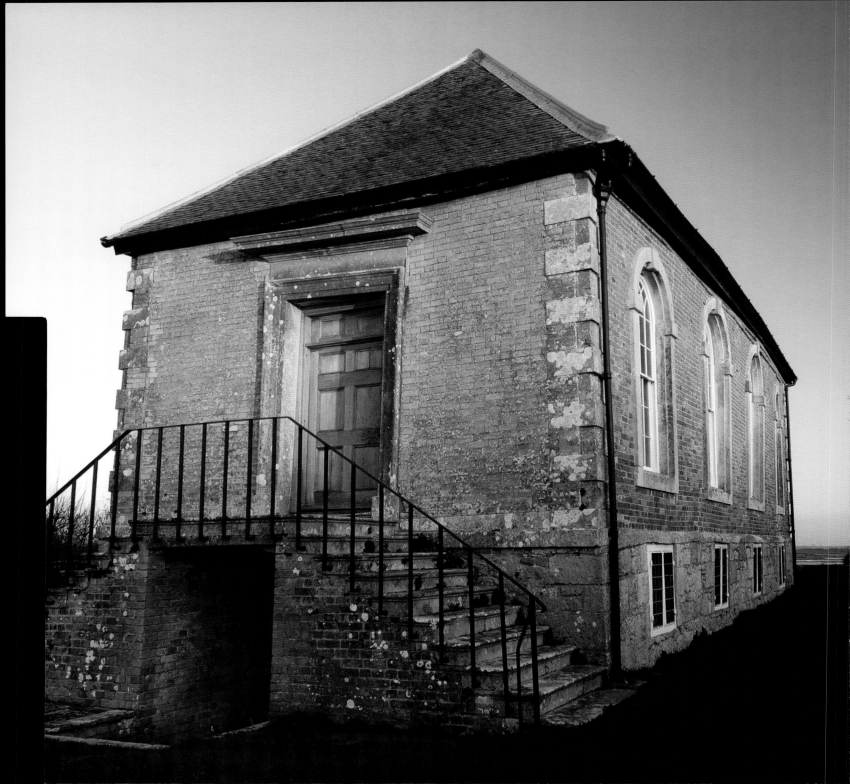

The historic Town Hall at Newtown lit by the first sun rays of the day.

J

An early morning view across to Gatcombe,
which was recorded in the *Domesday Book*.

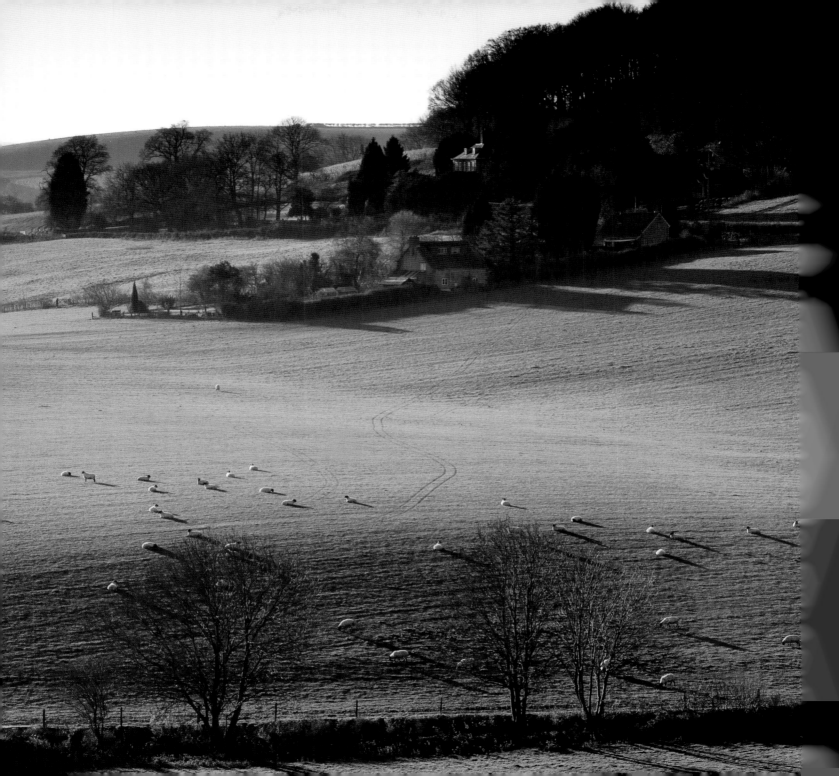

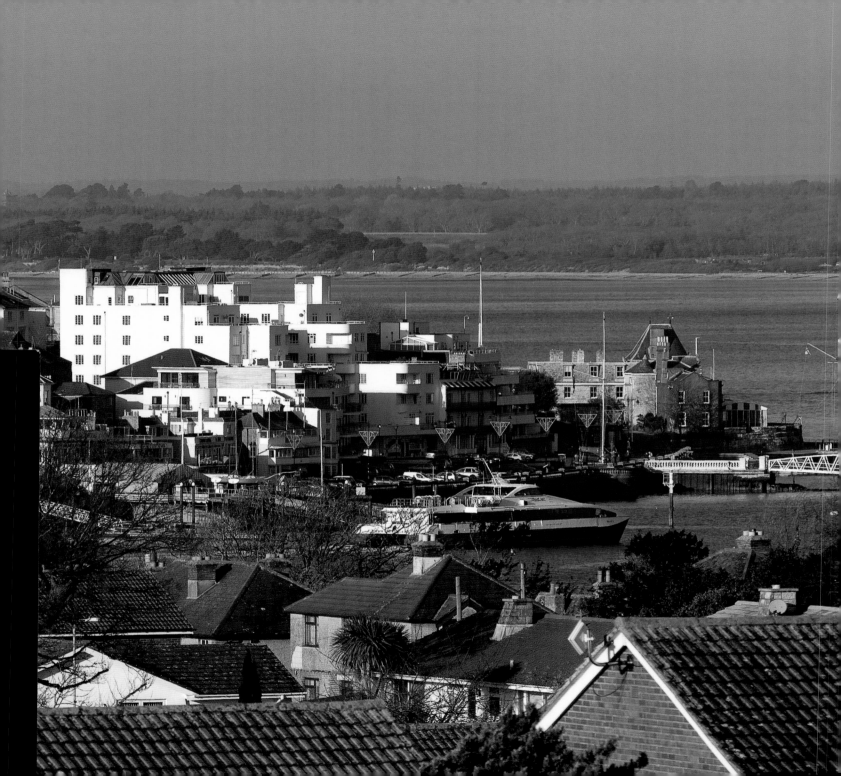

Looking over the rooftops to the river entrance at Cowes.

K

The busy quayside during Cowes Week with
sailing yachts racing in the background.

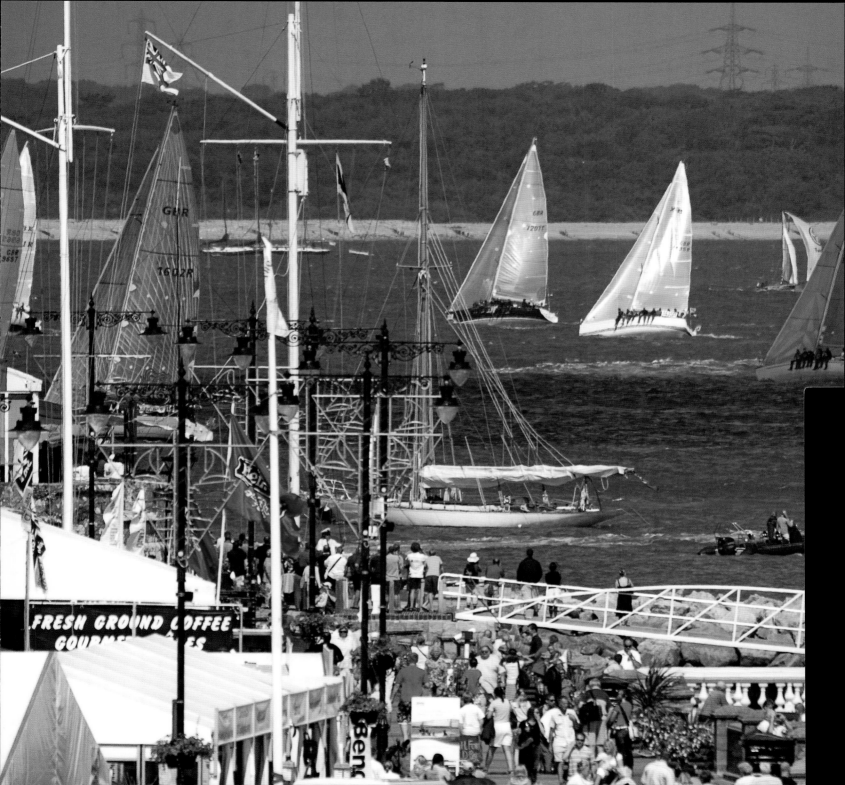

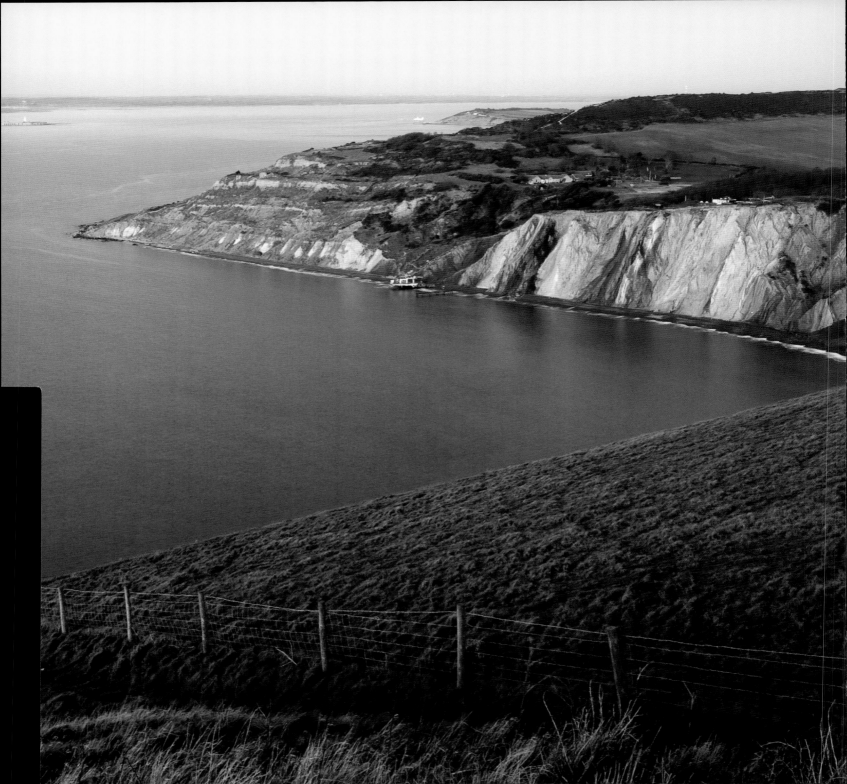

L

L

The colourful sands in the cliffs at Alum Bay, with Hurst Castle
and the Western Approaches to the Solent beyond.

L

L

L

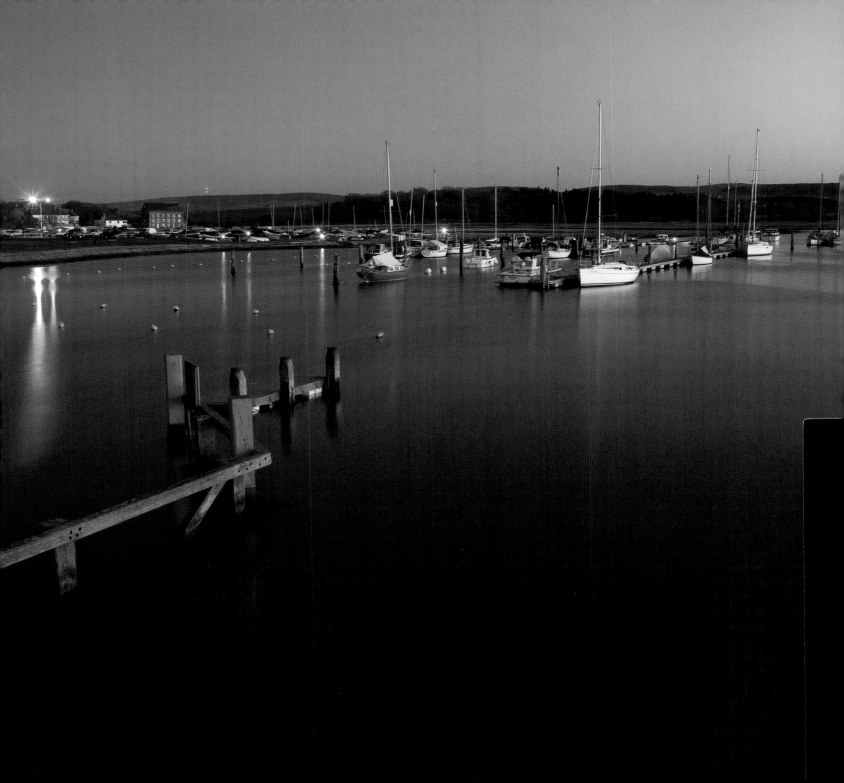

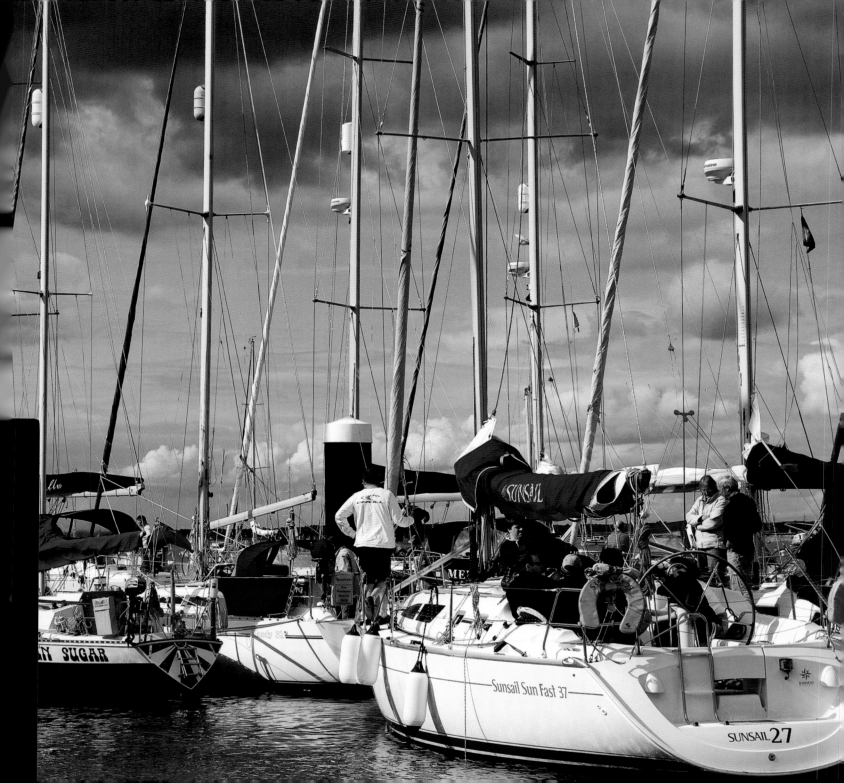

A busy evening at the yacht marina in Cowes.

M

M

M

A fisherman on the beach as yachts contesting
the Round the Island race pass by.

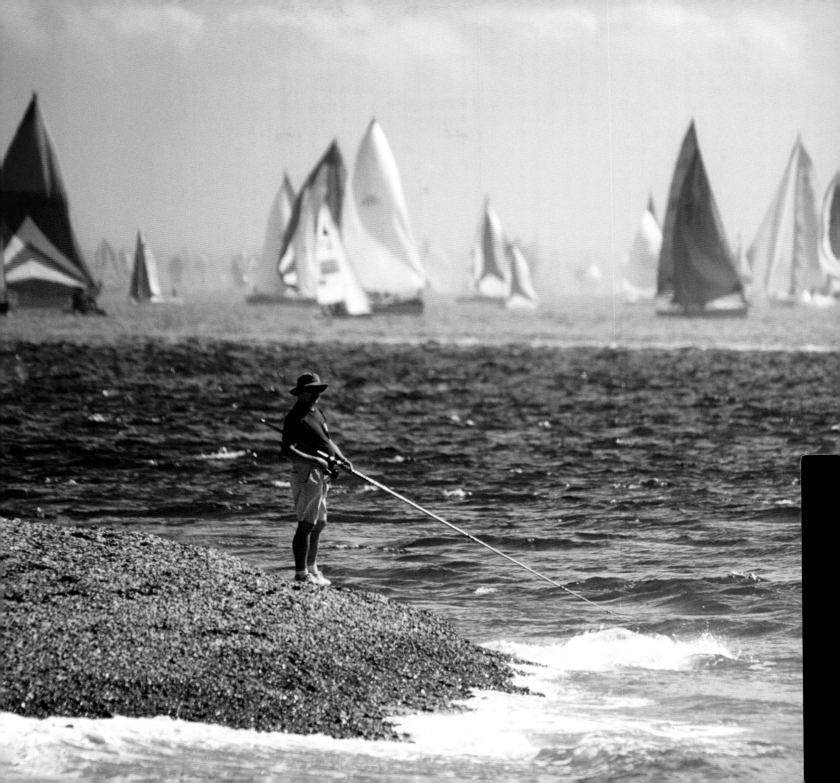

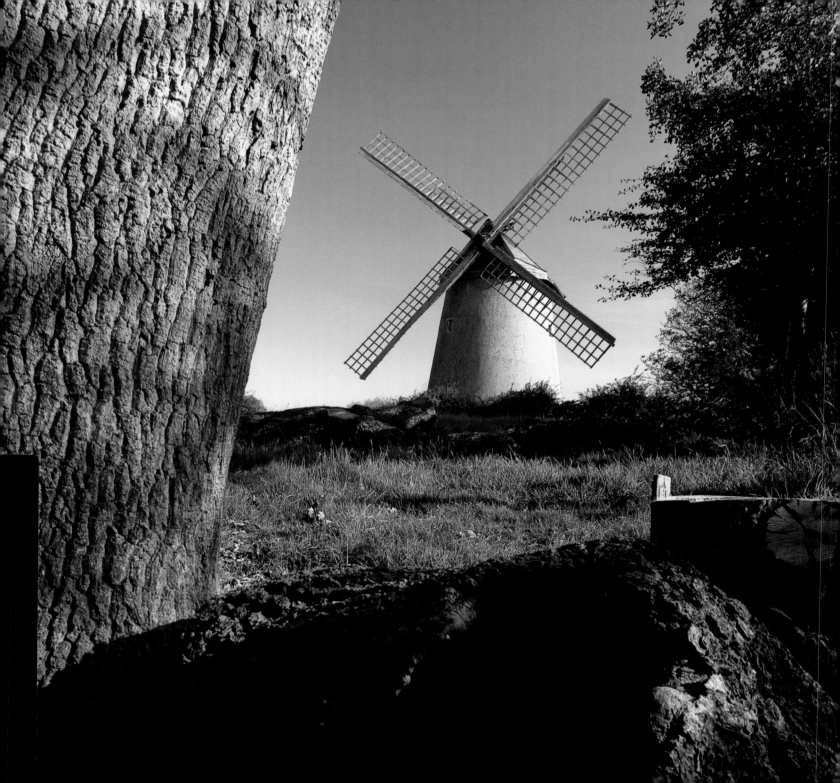

Looking up to the windmill at Bembridge.

N

Stormy skies and a rainbow over the ferry terminal at Cowes.

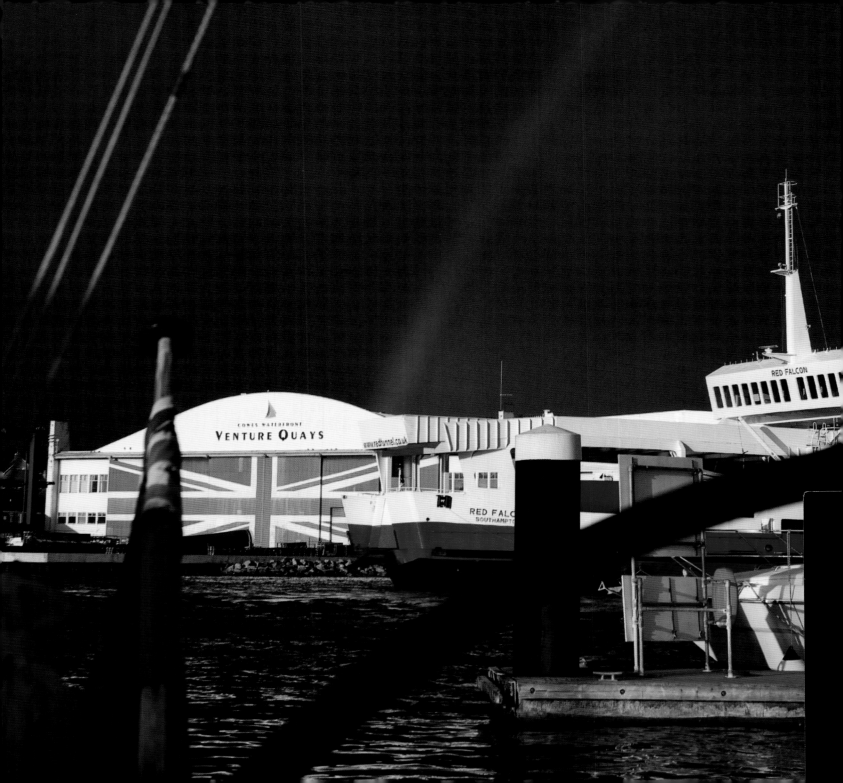

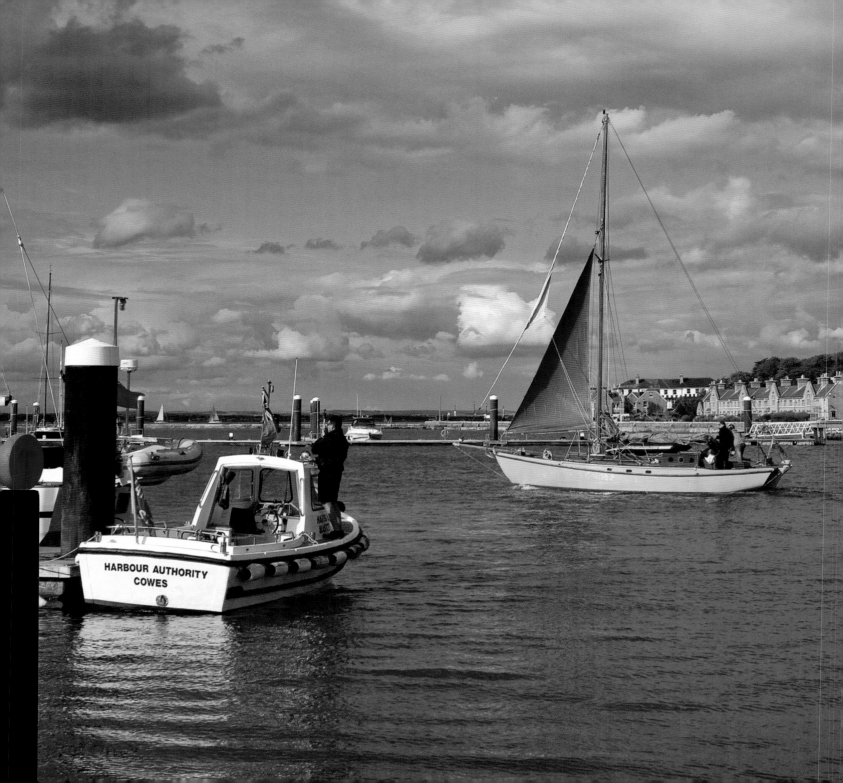

O

o

A classic yacht sails out of the River Medina at
Cowes past the Harbour Master's launch.

O

A melange of boats in the Solent during Cowes Week.

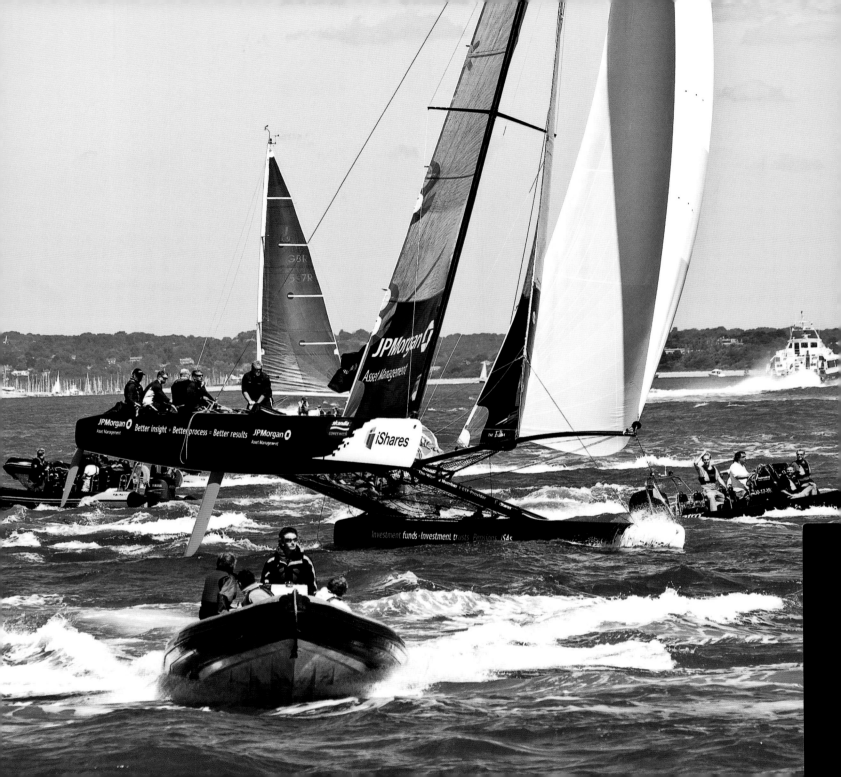

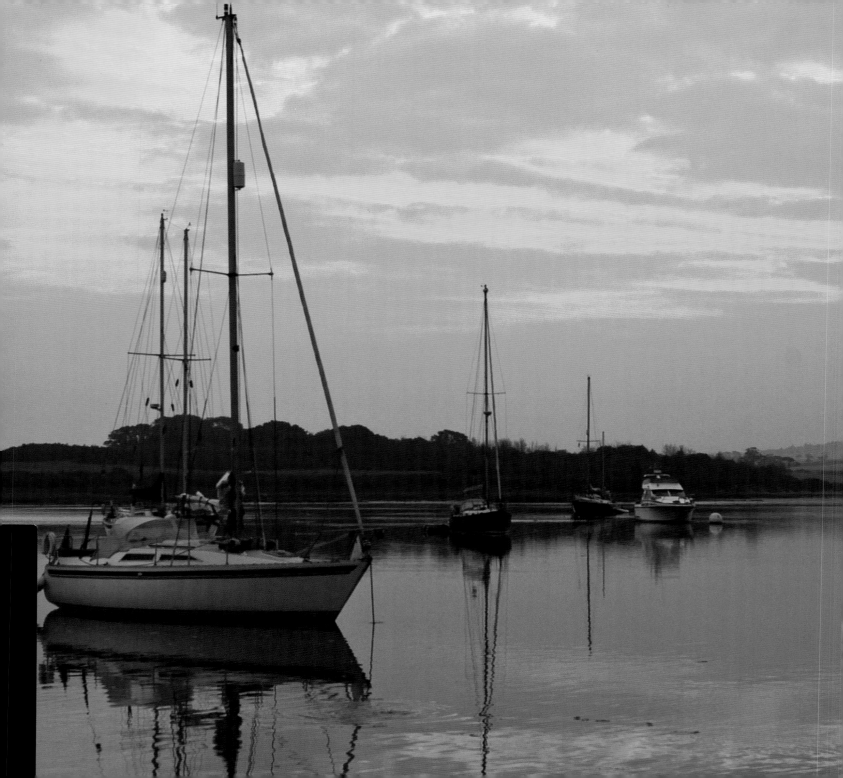

A moored sailing yacht in Newtown Creek before dawn with mist rising.

PQ

A stile on Stenbury Down looking out across fields towards Ventnor and the sea beyond.

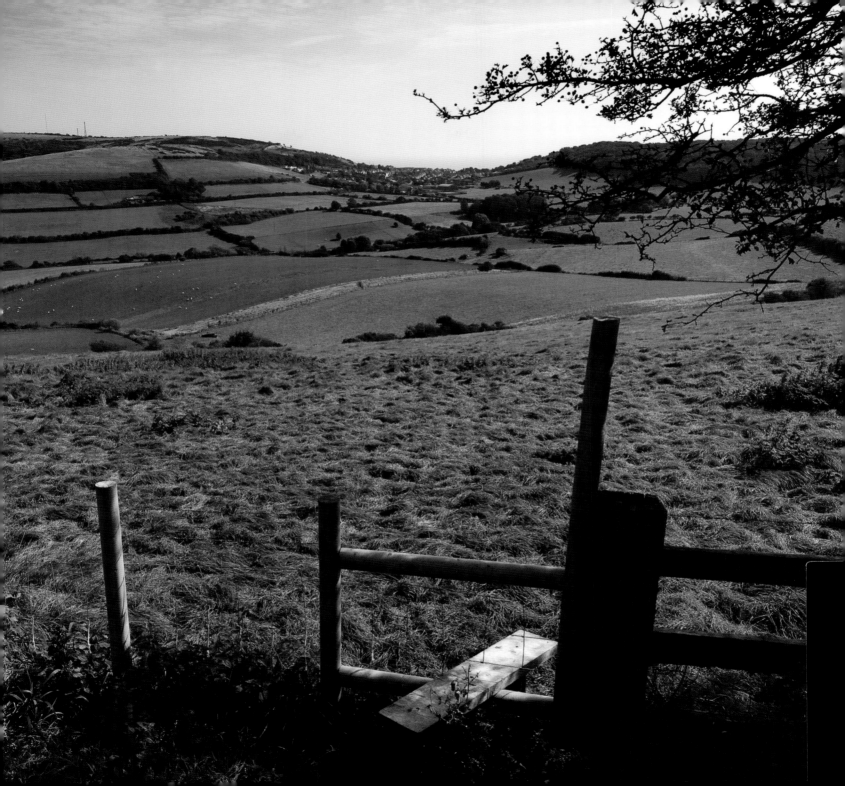

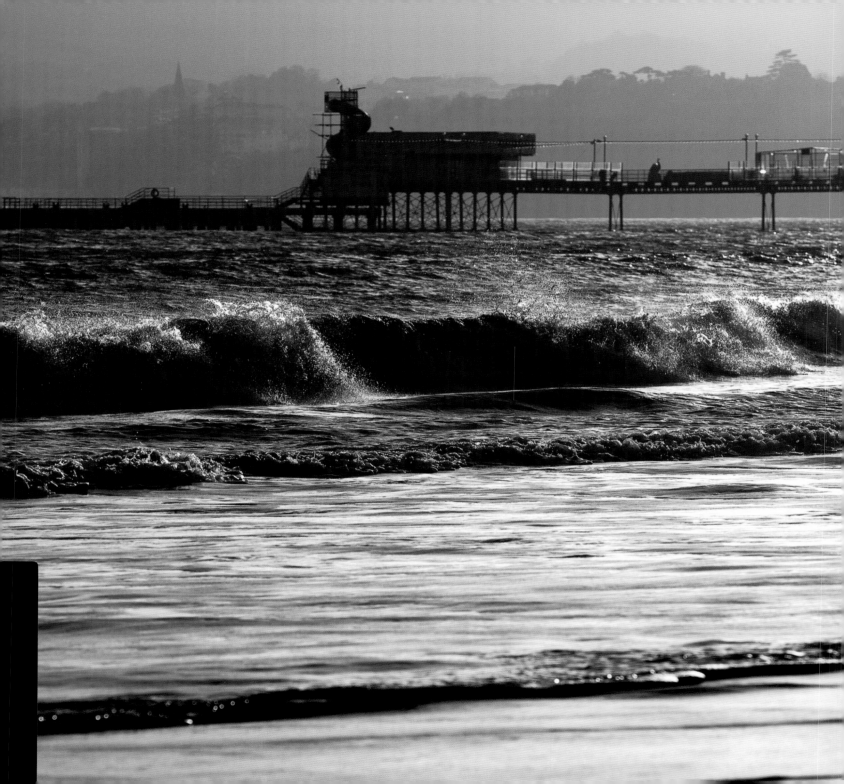

Crashing waves and a late afternoon sun looking out to Sandown Pier.

R

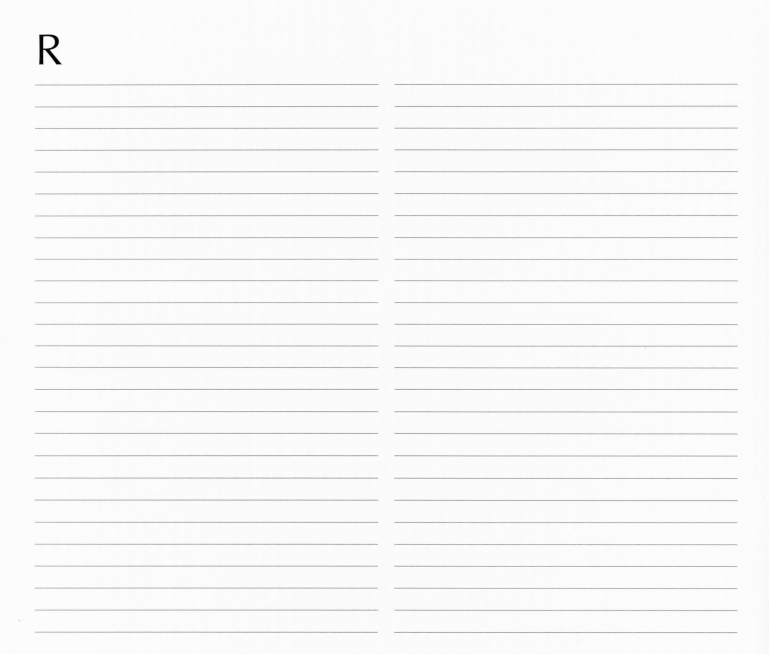

Picturesque Winkle Street in Calbourne Village.

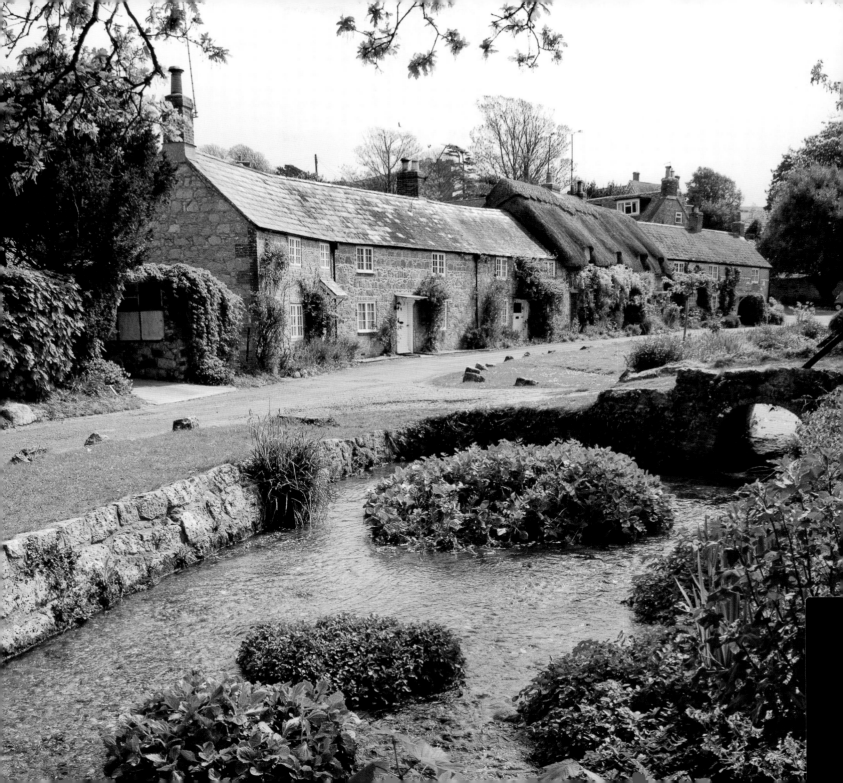

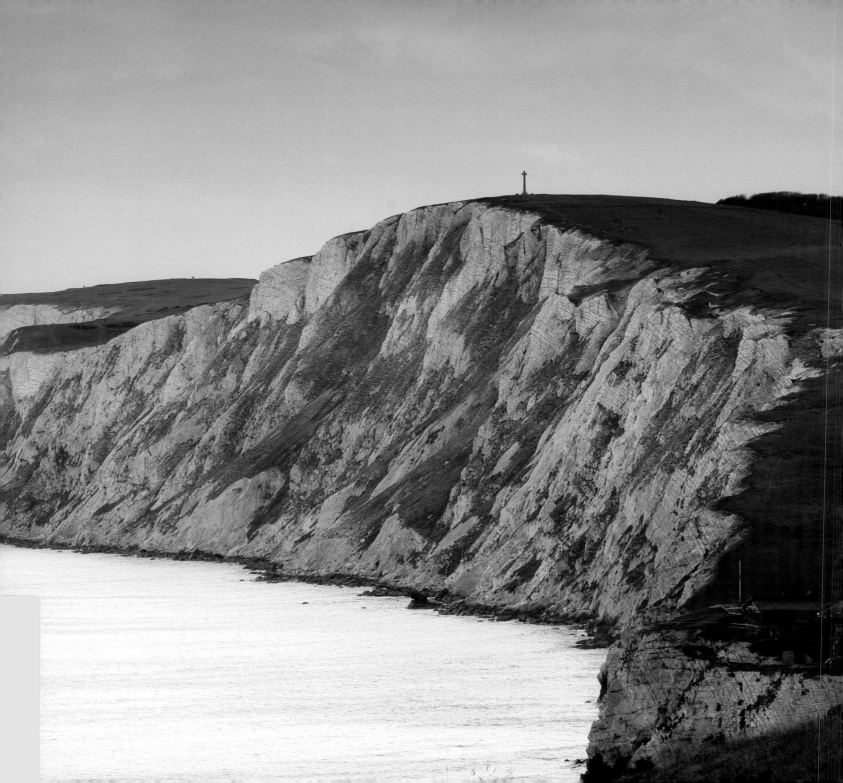

Looking over to Tennyson Down with people walking towards
the Tennyson monument, high on the eponymous downs.

S

S

S

Looking out across rough seas towards Castle Cove near Ventnor.

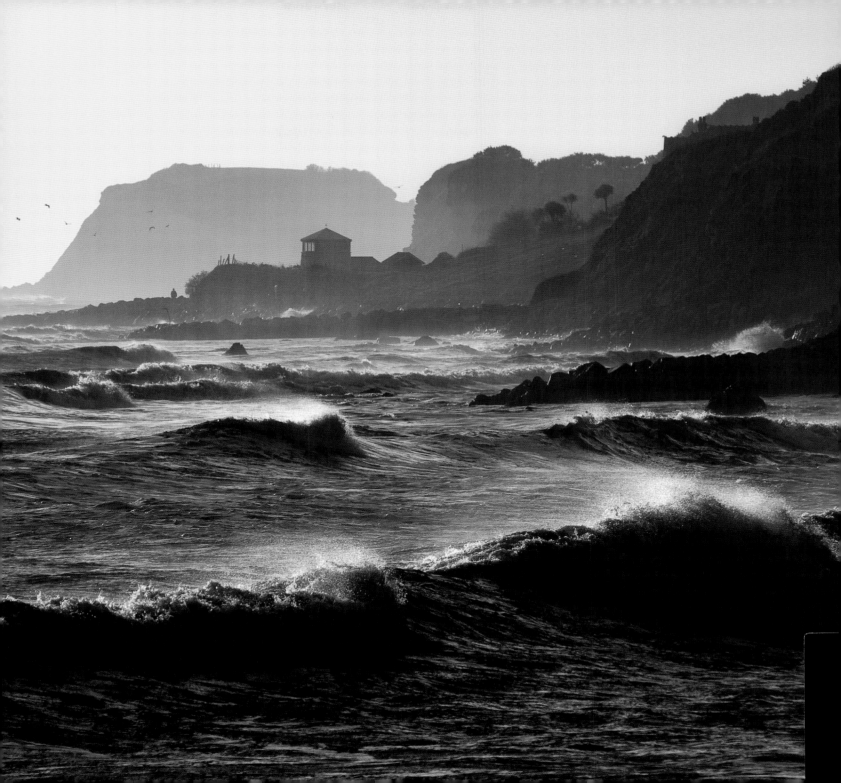

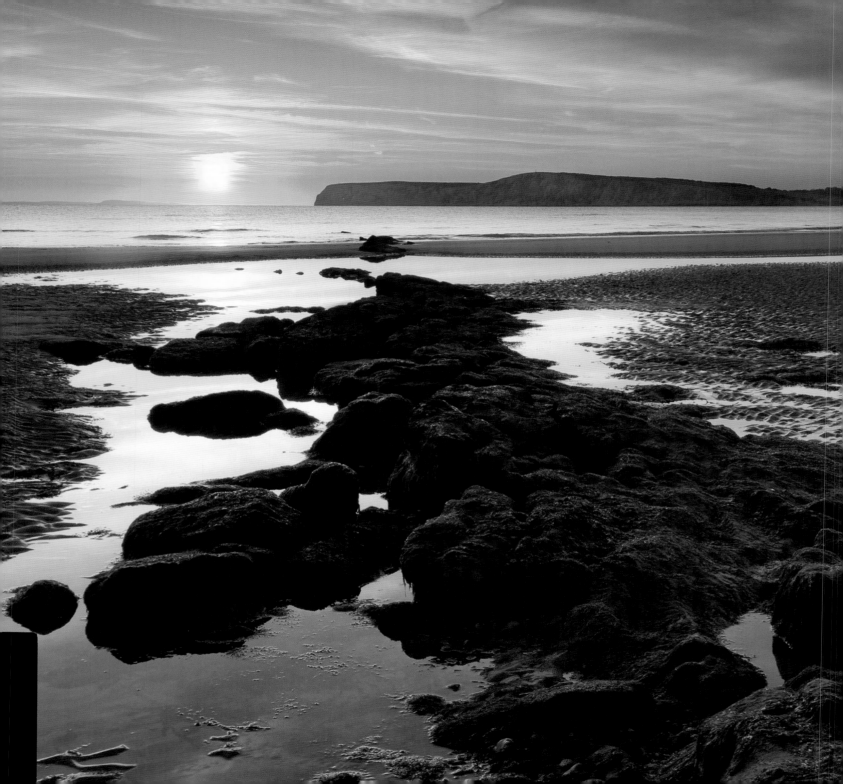

A setting sun over Tennyson Down viewed over
exposed rocks at low tide from Hanover Point.

T

A rural farmhouse near Whitwell.

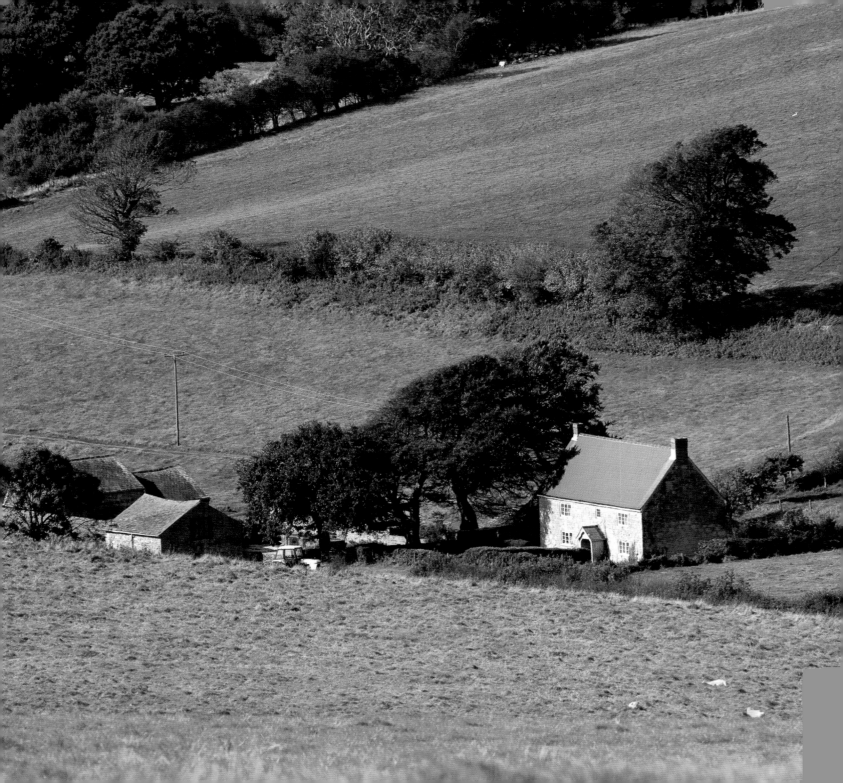

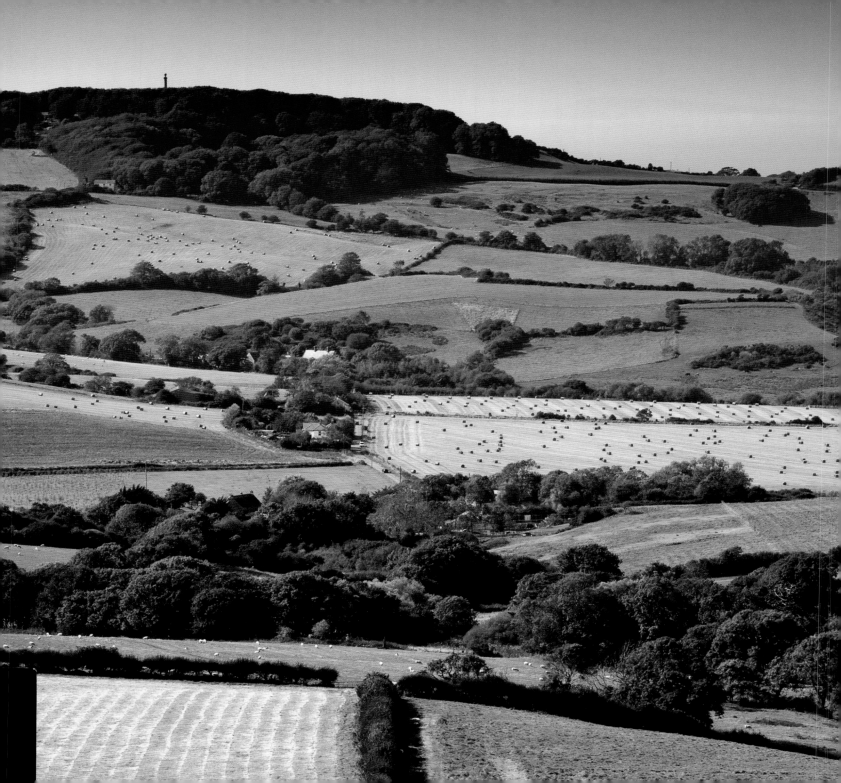

Stenbury Down looking over fields of hay bales to the coast.

UV

The quayside at Newport harbour at the head of the River Medina.

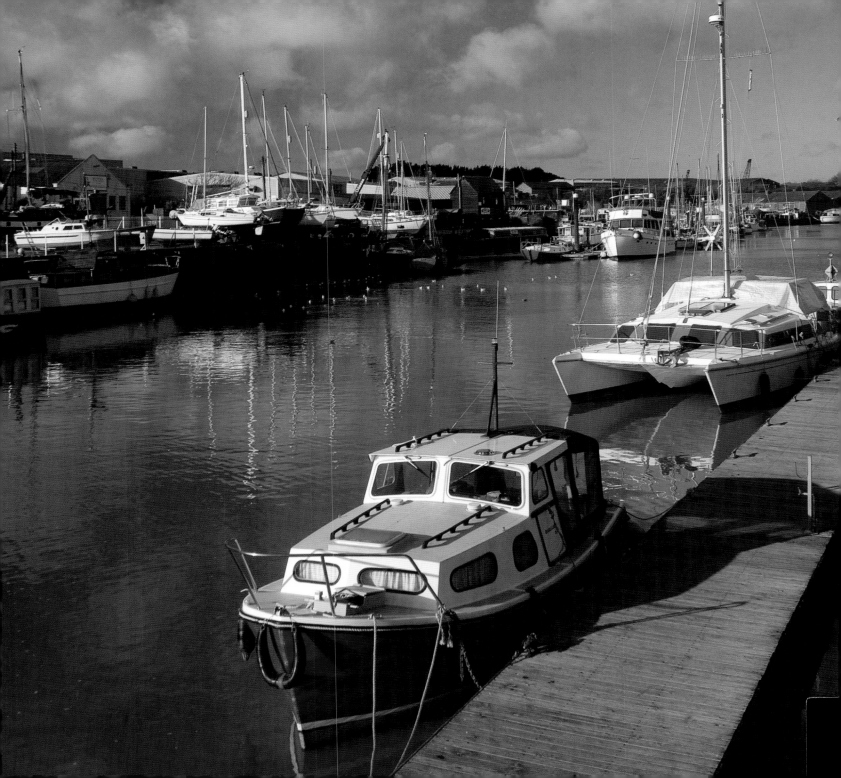

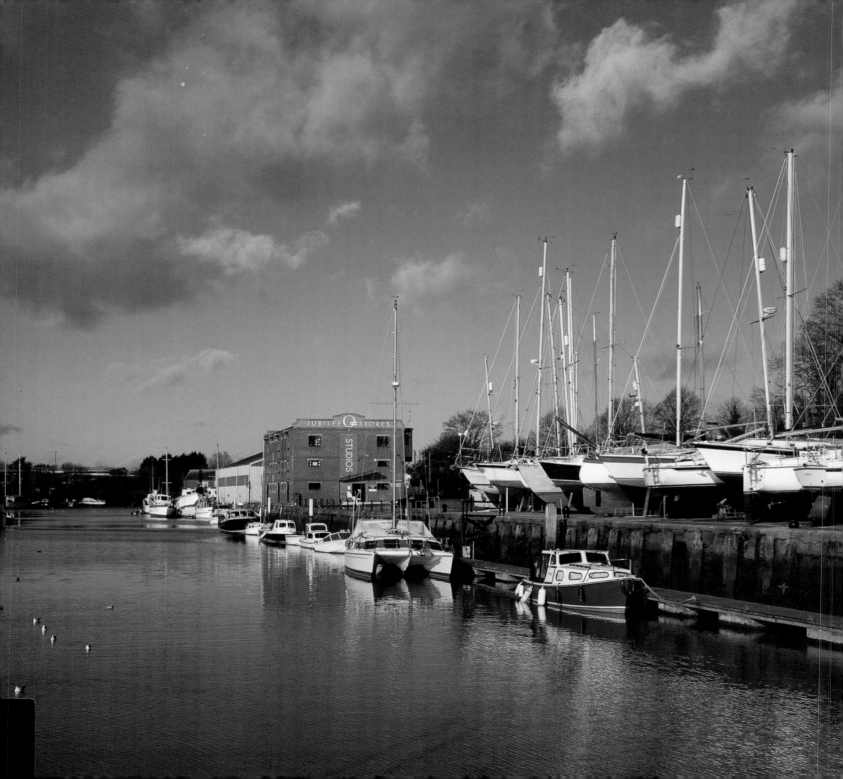

W

Sail and motor boats moored on the quayside at Newport harbour.

W

The bridge over the River Yar at Yarmouth at dusk.

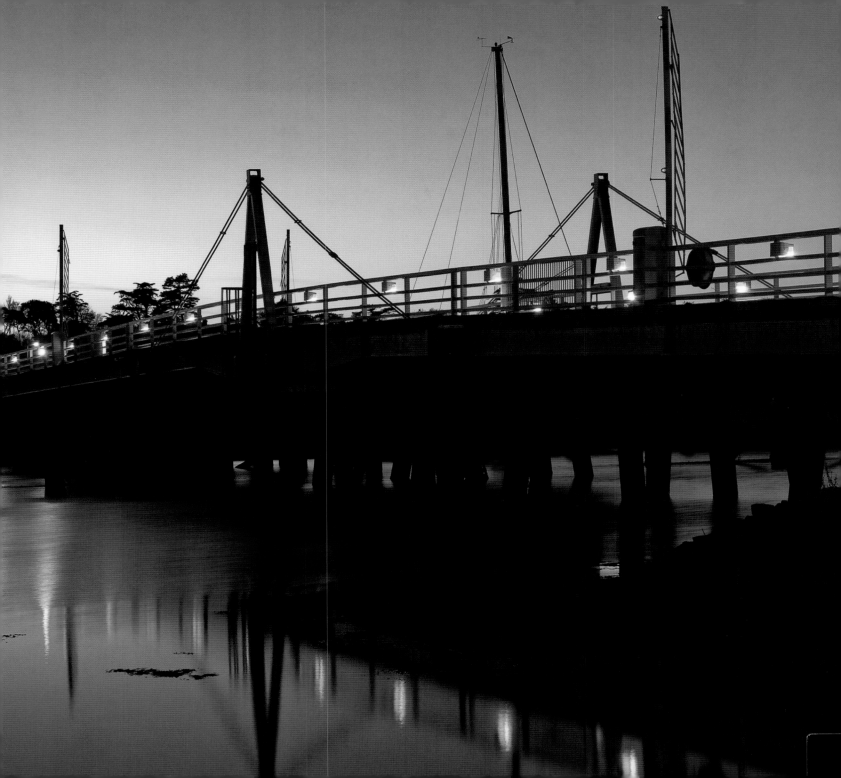

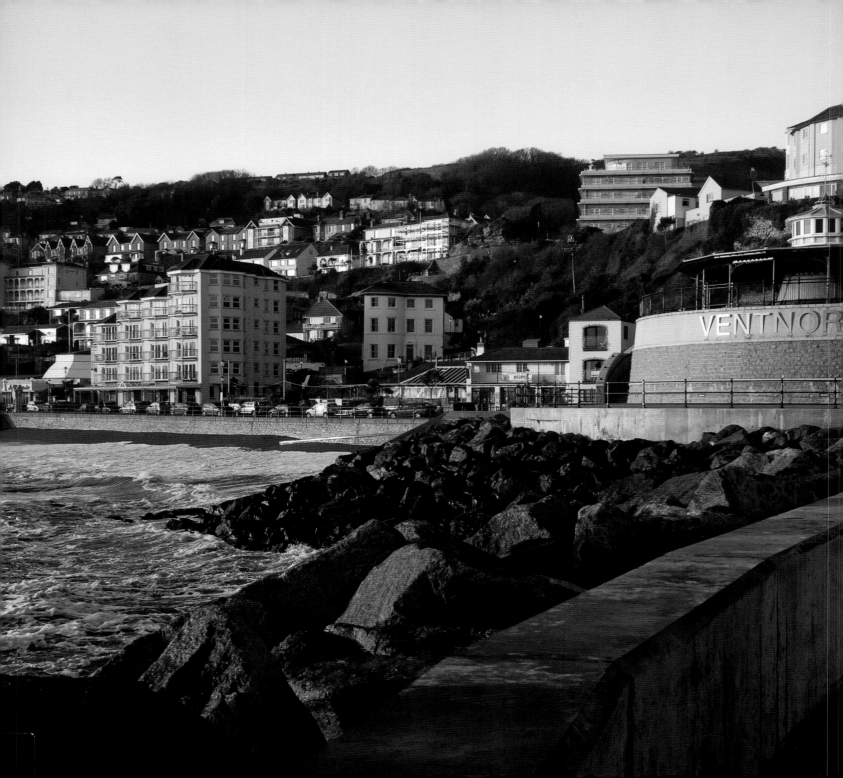

Looking back to Ventnor from the sea wall.

XYZ